Success Forces

JOSEPH SUGARMAN

Contemporary Books, Inc.
Chicago

Library of Congress Cataloging in Publication Data

Sugarman, Joseph, 1938–
   Success forces.

   1. Success.   I. Title.
HF5386.S889   650.1′4   80-65929
ISBN 0-8092-7061-7

Published by Contemporary Books, Inc.
180 North Michigan Avenue, Chicago, Illinois 60601
Manufactured in the United States of America
Library of Congress Catalog Card Number: 80-65929
International Standard Book Number: 0-8092-7061-7

Published simultaneously in Canada by
Beaverbooks
953 Dillingham Road
Pickering, Ontario L1W 1Z7
Canada

I would like to dedicate this book to several people who, all in their own way, contributed to the development of my Success Forces:

My wife, Wendy, who always urged me to bounce back after my disastrous failures and who stood by my side despite the many disappointments. She often had to single-handedly raise our children while I worked around the clock trying to build my business.

My secretary, and now executive vice-president, Mary Stanke, who never failed to support me during JS&A's roughest times. Her dedication, her self-taught skills, and her work ethic were a major contributing factor to JS&A's success and provided me with the freedom I needed to achieve my success.

Mary Stanke's staff—every one of them—for their dedication and effort and support of the principles of service to the consumer.

Special thanks also to my publisher, whose constant prodding kept me writing this book on airplanes, in airport terminals in Hong Kong and Hawaii, and late at night at home.

To my father, who in his own way made me realize that anything was possible with a positive attitude. And to my mother, who passed on to me her great sense of humor and raised my three great sisters. Unfortunately, she is not here to enjoy this book.

Finally, thanks to the many JS&A customers, without whose support and patronage there certainly would be no book.

Contents

Introduction   *ix*

Introduction

If you're thinking this is another one of those dumb success books, you're right. What makes this book different is that I am not your average success story. I'm a college dropout with a limited vocabulary and a whole bunch of failures to my credit. And even more incredible is that I have been able to make millions of dollars despite myself.

Now if you think that maybe I'm lucky, you're wrong. The truth is that I have probably failed more times than anybody reading this book.

But from all my failures, from all my dumb mistakes, I have discovered some interesting relationships.

I have discovered that there are actions we can take in the normal course of our lives that will greatly enhance our chances of success—actions that require very little effort and little change in our everyday routines.

Each of these actions automatically creates a "force." If you take the right action, the force will propel you toward success. Take the wrong action and you are forced closer toward failure.

Success Forces is a book designed to help you recognize these actions. Some of them you may already be following, achieving success despite yourself. Others you may not be following, failing without knowing why. And still others you may not realize exist.

Once you can recognize my Success Forces, your chances of success will start to increase despite yourself. With a little bit of conscientious effort, Success Forces will propel you to heights of success you've never dreamed possible.

I have distinguished myself by developing a successful business around the power of creativity. In the process of building my company I have discovered many truths. And I've discovered these truths not as a result of my successes, but from my failures.

I doubt very much that there are many people in business today who have failed more times at as many different things as I have. At times everything I touched turned to garbage. And from all these failures I learned things. And from all the things I've learned, I noticed that I could sort them into six philosophies—each with its own lesson.

I took these lessons and developed my own personal philosophy called "Success Forces." Whenever I succeeded, I found I had been following my philosophies. Whenever I failed, I was violating these same philosophies.

I then started to reveal my Success Forces at speeches I gave throughout the country. I noticed people taking notes. It wasn't until a few years after those first speeches that I started getting letters from people telling me that my Success Forces worked. One letter told me how I had changed a person's life. Another told me how someone had profited as a direct result of my speech.

Then I started to publish my Success Forces, because people were asking for copies of my speeches and soon, from the encouragement of many of these people, I decided to write this book. That's how *Success Forces* evolved.

Before I achieved my own success, I read all the success books and interviewed successful people. I had great dreams of success. I knew that one day I, too, would be successful—despite my failures—and that success would not come because of the books I had read or the people I had met. I knew I had to discover on my own the real forces that seemed to propel people to great success, despite themselves, while others seemed to fail no matter how hard they tried.

Some of my Success Forces may strike you as very elementary and others as complete surprises. That's fine. But don't underestimate any of the six forces I present. Each one can be a powerful influence in your life if you'll accept my premise.

Do they work? What forces take place, and what can we do to make these forces work for us? What very simple basic things can we do in our lives that will *force* us to be more successful despite ourselves?

That's the entire idea of this book. *Success Forces* is a simple program that can be followed almost subconsciously. Any single Success Force will work. Harness all of them and your chances of success will be greatly enhanced.

Remember, I'm not an author who writes about success and then makes a fortune from the sale of my book. I've made my fortune and the techniques I've used have worked for me time and time again. Even if you've read all the success books ever written, this book will give you a totally different perspective.

The one thing I don't give you is a step-by-step "formula" or a "plan" or a "secret" method. I believe in the old adage, "Feed a man fish and he will eat for a day; teach a man to fish and he will eat for a lifetime." I'm not going to feed you a fish, a formula, or false hopes. *Success Forces* is my first book. It's a book that took me almost twenty-five years of failure to write.

Success Forces is not a book about marketing. It's not a book about the mail order industry, and although I use a few examples from my business experience, it's not a book about business. I don't even use big words—mainly because I don't know many.

I did little research for this book, so you won't find extensive footnotes with references to great philosophers. Instead, I am expressing my personal philosophies—philosophies that I have developed after literally years of failures and successes.

I have developed these philosophies from my experiences and then observed them actually working. I have constantly questioned their validity; challenged them, only to discover a consistency that has made me believe that the philosophies I teach in this book do indeed work.

There is little that will be revolutionary and little that can be considered a breakthrough with the exception of the way I present this information. By presenting my concepts as "forces" and showing you how to use them to be successful, I provide the basis for a new perspective on success, motivation, and self-improvement.

Success Forces is my contribution to your success. It will work for you and, even more important, you'll be a lot happier as a result.

SECTION I

1
The Start

Before we discuss my philosophies, I'd like you to get to know me, to learn about some of my failures and the path that led me to this book. That's what Section I of my book is all about. After all, my advice won't be worth very much if you don't know how I developed my concept.

I was born on Chicago's west side on April 25, 1938, and I eventually had three younger sisters—Barbara, Nancy, and Judy.

Our family moved from Chicago to Oak Park, Illinois, when I was three and back to Chicago and then back to Oak Park when I was twelve years old. Oak Park is a small suburb due west of Chicago.

My father was in the printing equipment business. He was the president of his firm, Consolidated Photo Engraving and Equipment Company, which manufactured printing equipment and large process cameras for the printing and platemaking industry.

I can remember sitting at the kitchen table when I was three years old and watching my father read the newspaper. Suddenly he'd come to an advertisement and would show it to me saying, "Joey, look at this terrific ad." Later I would look at newspapers to see if I could find some "terrific ads." My interest in advertising never left me.

When I was eight years old, I lived in the Albany Park section of Chicago with my family in a three-story six-flat apartment.

On a beautiful warm summer afternoon my mom gave me twelve cents to catch the one o'clock movie at the Terminal Theatre. John Wayne was the hero in a rugged western in which the cowboys had to camp out, light campfires, and cook their meals.

After the movie I stepped out into the bright afternoon sun. I squinted as my eyes slowly adjusted to the brightness, and I walked the two blocks toward home.

Lawrence Avenue was filled with small shops. It was 1946 and as I strolled down the street, streetcars clanked down the tracks of Lawrence Avenue.

Home was only a few blocks away. There was the delicatessen where my parents used to order corned beef sandwiches. Then came the corner tobacco shop at Kimball and Lawrence where my mom used to buy her cigarettes. And the rapid transit train to downtown Chicago terminated at the same corner.

I turned north. Home was only half a block away. I walked past a few six-flats, around the side of my apartment building to the backyard, and then up the stairs to the back door.

There was nothing much to do that day. School was out for the summer, my mom was busy around the apartment, and I had the rest of the day to keep busy. I couldn't forget that scene by the campfire. John Wayne was my favorite cowboy and I had seen practically every movie he played in.

I took my squirt gun and holster from a hallway closet, put them on and went into the kitchen, where I filled my squirt gun and sneaked a pack of matches that was lying in a cupboard drawer.

I went down the stairs, through the backyard, and down the alley behind my house to an abandoned garage located in an empty lot at the end of my block. The garage had no doors or windows. Everything had withered, decayed, or been removed long ago. A piece of the roof hung precariously from the roof supports. A strong gust would certainly collapse the garage one of these days, and we were often warned not to play around it.

I went inside the garage and decided to make a small campfire. I gathered a few loose bricks, made a circle like the one I had seen in the movie, and gathered some twigs and paper to start a small fire.

With the matches, I lit the fire and watched it just about burn out.

I took out my squirt gun, took careful aim and spat; there was a puff of smoke and the fire was extinguished. That was fantastic. I had to do it again. But this time I decided to make a bigger fire.

I increased the size of my brick fireplace, put a lot more paper and twigs inside. I was looking for twigs on the side of the garage and saw that somebody had cut down a tree and left some thick green branches.

I thought I'd use the green branches to help me smother the next fire. Well, the fire was a beauty. And to make my adventure even more exciting, I scattered the burning twigs all over the garage with a stick. Pretty soon little fires were burning all over the garage. The garage walls looked as if they were about to catch on fire. There were flames everywhere.

Me worry? Not on your life. I quickly stepped into action. I went outside the garage, took the biggest, lushest green branch I could find, and with John Wayne action, ran from fire to fire, smothering them with force and determination.

As the last of the fires were put out and the twigs smoldered, I took out my squirt gun, took aim and poof—out went the smoldering twigs. Boy, was that exciting. I felt like an eight-year-old John Wayne.

But I didn't stop there. There was a pretty young girl named

Robin who lived upstairs in our apartment building. I liked Robin, but she wasn't so impressed with me.

Robin liked the boy next door—an eight-year-old boy named Gene Rocklin. Gene was a bookworm—one of those gifted children who sat down and read everything he could get his hands on. He was already into Shakespeare while I was still stumbling through Dick and Jane.

I can remember my mother always saying, "Why can't you read like Gene next door?" And I can remember Robin telling me how she really liked boys who were as smart as Gene. No question about it, Gene and his brain were the talk of our apartment building.

I was so impressed with the John Wayne valor that I had exhibited in the face of danger from the out-of-control fire that I decided to impress Robin with my bravery.

I didn't just walk home. I strutted, my legs bowed, my six-gun at my side. I walked up to Robin's door. "Robin," I shouted, "come here, I've got something to show you."

When Robin appeared, I beamed. "Robin, I've got something to show you that you'll never forget. Robin, you'll love what I'm about to do. Be ready in ten minutes. OK?"

While I was waiting for Robin, I rushed back to the garage and set up the bricks for the biggest fire ever. I gathered twigs, wood, paper—everything I could get my hands on. I took the stick I had used to spread the fire and put it against the side of the garage. I hid those lush green branches just outside the garage on a little hill where neighbors often dumped their garbage. I placed the biggest, lushest green branch right at the top, where it would be ready for me to grab at the very last moment.

I ran home, raced into the house and filled up my squirt gun. I got a big hanky and wrapped it around my neck like a cowboy's bandana and went up to Robin.

She appeared in a white dress with a ribbon in her hair. She was pretty—the sugar and spice little girls are supposed to be made of—and I wasn't ashamed to admit that I really liked her.

Of course, I'd never tell her that. She liked Gene. I didn't have a chance. Or did I? I might be able to impress her with my demonstration of strength and fierce determination in my battle against the forces of fire and evil.

Robin followed me to the garage, drawn by my obvious enthusiasm. I took her inside where my large campfire was already prepared.

I turned to Robin and blurted, "Now Robin, I don't want you to get excited or cry or anything. Just know that I've always got things under control."

I lit the fire as Robin stood back a little, still curious about what I was doing. The fire started to burn and it really was big. Robin still looked puzzled.

Then, as the fire was reaching its peak, I told Robin to step outside the garage as I reached confidently for the stick. With the stick I threw the burning debris all over the garage.

Now the flames were all over, lapping at the garage walls. It was the biggest fire yet and almost looked as if it were out of control.

I glanced at Robin. She looked frightened. I shouted, "Don't worry, Robin, I'll save you." I then raced outside the garage to pick up one of those nice thick, lush green branches only to discover they were gone. The garbage truck must have hauled them away.

There it was, my chance to impress Robin: the fire out of control and Robin looking at me as if she thought I was nuts.

I did the only thing left to do. I pulled out my squirt gun. But it was too late. The garage burned down. Robin ran home to tell her parents and I could just imagine what she must have thought.

When the fire truck arrived, I was there, my squirt gun empty and my mother dragging me home by the ears.

I was punished. You'd rather expect that. But I didn't expect Robin to hide every time I went out to play. I thought that was unfair. And Gene, the creep, avoided me too.

I had learned my lesson—a lesson I'd never forget. For this is a lesson that applies to my business philosophy even to this day.

Think about it. How many people build bigger and bigger fires, only to find that one day they are unable to put them out? Soon the fire consumes them.

I've always had a lush green branch in my hand whenever I start a fire. I never leave one outside. I always have an out whenever I do something that might consume me. I learned my lesson well.

Robin eventually married someone while she attended college. I'm sure she'll always remember me—probably more so than Gene.

Gene graduated first in his class in college. I don't know what he does now. I really don't care. I still think he's a creep.

2
The Promoter

In grammar school my favorite activity was writing. I'd write a story and if I was called on to read it, I would crack up the class. Back in sixth grade I was the class humorist.

In sixth grade I also had my first tastes of the business world. My father helped me set up a small printing business. He bought me a printing press, type, and a small proof press. I paid for the equipment with time payments and earned enough money to pay for the equipment and have a little extra money.

That year I also invented a small game that I brought to my father's patent attorney for a patent to protect it. The attorney also prepared a letter explaining the game so I could present it to the Parker Brothers Game Company.

The game was never accepted and the printing business soon became rather boring. But both were my first experiences in business.

At Oak Park and River Forest High School I joined the

school's photo staff and newspaper and started writing my own stories, adding my own photos.

The school frowned on humor, so I didn't get much of a chance to use it, but I did write many stories and was the school's sports photographer, which got me to the sidelines of many of Oak Park's big sports events.

High school was probably one of the most exciting times of my life. Ernest Hemingway was a former student at Oak Park High, Frank Lloyd Wright had taught there, and the school was steeped with tradition going back well into the 1880s.

In 1956, my senior year at Oak Park, I was getting frustrated with the limits placed on my writing by the very conservative school paper and decided to put out my own with my father's help and encouragement. I organized all the top writers at the school and even used our star basketball players to ensure that all of us wouldn't be dismissed from school.

The paper was published and was a great success. Despite a few close calls with the faculty, I graduated.

I enrolled at the University of Illinois in journalism, although my father had hoped I would choose engineering, since this was the area that would help him the most in his business. College was supposed to groom me to take over my father's company when he retired.

During that summer I convinced my father to buy me a beautiful 1956 racing Corvette. It was the first of a new breed of Corvettes that was introduced at the Sebring race in Florida.

All prepared to go to Illinois, I discovered that they didn't allow cars there the first year, and here I had this beautiful Corvette. So I worked for part of the summer and decided to take my last fling by driving down to Florida for a final summer vacation.

I had a few relatives who lived in Miami, and I was to stay with them. After spending a week in the beautiful Florida sunshine, I realized that attending the University of Miami made a lot more sense than attending the University of Illinois, so I compromised with my father and enrolled at the University of Miami's Electrical Engineering School. I had always liked electronic gadgets and radio communications even though writing was my first love.

In college I joined a fraternity, Phi Sigma Delta, and spent two years getting average grades until my father asked me to help him run his New York office. He was having rough times during the 1958 recession and needed my help.

He owned a two-story office building in a poor section of town off 8th Avenue on 26th Street. There used to be ten people in the office but everybody quit or was fired during this period. I offered to work for him for nothing and acted as his salesman and serviceman even though I knew nothing about servicing printing equipment.

Despite my handicaps, I did manage to get by, and eventually I hired a few people and got the office functioning again.

During this time my father approached me with an idea. The Printing Industry of America was staging a printing exposition in New York, and they had reserved the New York Coliseum. Space at the show went so fast that almost all the foreign companies were prevented from showing their products. My father suggested that I book the nearby New York Trade Show Building and stage my own show for the foreign companies that couldn't get space in the other show and for Americans who also wanted to exhibit.

It sounded like a great idea, so I reserved the New York Trade Show Building, called my exhibition Spectra '59, designed a full-color poster, a brochure and a space application form, and sent it to all the foreign and American manufacturers.

Responses started to come in, but not as fast as I had hoped. The advertising materials looked very professional and were more exciting than those for the major show at the Coliseum. We actually looked like the major show in the eyes of the Europeans and Japanese.

But I was twenty years old at the time and looked so young that if a potential exhibitor would meet me he would not have confidence that I could succeed. I couldn't use my father as the sponsor because he was competition for most of the exhibitors I wanted to attract.

The printing bills were starting to come due so I had to take some positive action. I hired a sixty-five-year-old actor who looked as distinguished as the chairman of the board of any top U.S. corporation, and I told him which lines to use. He was to be my personal representative. Whenever I'd get a call from an interested party who wanted to discuss the show in more detail, I'd simply inform him in a slow yet deep voice that I was too busy and that I would send my personal representative.

When things started to build and the sales started coming in, I called a college buddy of mine, Richard Pieper, and asked him if he'd like to help me out. He agreed and came up for the summer. He would handle the promotion and I would handle the sales.

Then I went to Europe to close a few deals that were pending. I know I must have shocked a few people. By this time I had turned twenty-one, but I probably looked more like eighteen, and my grey-haired actor was performing on Broadway and couldn't spare the time to travel to Europe for me.

Nevertheless, we managed to turn Spectra '59 into a very successful exhibition. The five floors of the New York Trade Show Building were sold out, we attracted a large crowd, and everybody was happy.

The exhibitors were pleased, the visitors were pleased, and even the unions that ripped off the exhibitors were pleased. Dick Pieper and I ended up with nothing. We had spent our last pennies promoting the show and had nothing to show for our efforts other than plenty of experience.

But who cared? We had a lot of fun, learned what the real world was all about, and everybody benefited. Dick joined his father's small electrical contracting business back in Milwaukee and built it into a very successful company. I went back to school. Things sure seemed quieter.

3
The Rise and Fall
of Joe Subway

After a taste of the real world, college took on real meaning for me. I was now a more serious student. My grades improved dramatically and I spent less time on social activities.

I dropped out of the fraternity house and rented an apartment off campus. During my stay at the apartment, I studied at the kitchen table every evening. Keeping the radio playing softly in the background, I listened to Bob Greene on Miami radio station WINZ. I learned how to concentrate on my studies despite the radio, which would play the novelty and hit rock and roll songs of the late fifties.

One evening at a party I met Neil Sedaka, a rock singer who had cut a couple of records and then rose to the top of the charts. He was a regular sort of guy who told me how he really hated the music he sang, but because of its commercial success, it made it possible for him to occasionally play and sing the music he really enjoyed.

After meeting him, and knowing every rock and novelty tune on the music charts, the idea of writing my own song and singing it really appealed to me. Here was an average guy from Brooklyn, not especially good looking, who was the hit of the party. Girls were chasing him; he had plenty of money and he was living a very exciting and interesting life. Why couldn't I do the same?

The key, of course, was a hit record. I had to write one first. I had already written lyrics for a song during my stay in New York, around the time of several successful space flights by American astronauts. The song was called "Santa's Got a Problem," and the theme was quite topical. What if Americans soon lived on the moon? How would Santa deliver toys? "Santa's got a problem, for very very soon, good girls and boys would want their toys delivered to the moon." So the song went. A great idea, I thought—until I tried to sell it. Despite many weeks of knocking on doors in New York, I couldn't interest anybody.

I met Archie Bleyer, the band leader who also managed the Everly Brothers. We were on a plane to Europe where I was trying to sell exhibition space for Spectra '59. He told me how impossible it was to sell a record, let alone a seasonal song like mine. Despite my setbacks, I was determined not to give up.

During a break from school in 1960, I met an old high school friend, Dick Bjork. Dick was an excellent piano player who was always the hit of any high school party. I convinced him to write some music for my Santa song and a few other novelty songs I had written while at school.

I wrote a song, "Is It Chilly in Chile during Christmas?" The weather, of course, was warm during the cold Christmas season in the U.S. I needed a flip hit for my Santa space song and it fit the bill perfectly.

Then I wrote a novelty tune that played to a calypso beat called "Mudder Goose." It was simply an up-to-date rendition of the Mother Goose nursery rhymes had they been written in 1960. Some examples:

Hickory Dickory Dock. The mouse ran up the clock. The clock struck one and blew up. It was a time bomb.

Little Miss Muffet sat on her tuffet eating some curds and whey. Along came a spider and sat down beside her and said, "Like what's happening?"

[Chorus] Mother Goose was a very hip poet. She was hip but we didn't know it. It wasn't 'til later years that her modern version made our ears.

Dick collaborated with me in writing the music and I brought to Miami the music charts and a tape we recorded. I then contacted a local recording studio and told them that I wanted to record my songs. I didn't need musical accompaniment as I had the recording of Dick playing the piano.

When I arrived at the recording studio they gave me Studio A, and I pulled out my music. I had never sung before in my life. They rolled my music tape and I started to sing "Santa's Got a Problem." From the expressions in the control booth, I was convinced I was not doing a very good job. There was agony written on the face of the engineer, who stepped out of the control booth and spent two hours trying to get me to sing the song correctly. Finally we resorted to singing it several times and he would very carefully splice sentences, words, phrases—anything that would sound right—into a single tape.

It was a rather humiliating experience that convinced me that I definitely was not naturally endowed with much of a voice. Frank Sinatra certainly had nothing to worry about. Finally, after another two hours, the engineer realized that the song wasn't going to sound like much unless I had a professional singer. He politely suggested that he could get me a singer to cut the record if I wanted. As I was really only cutting a demo record anyway, I agreed, and after lunch a local nightclub performer showed up and sang my two Christmas songs. He was able to do them in a matter of minutes.

I still insisted on doing my "Mudder Goose" song because the nursery rhymes were not sung but rather recited in a rather stupid-sounding way. I was perfect for that.

Early the next summer, in 1961, after school let out, I took my records, or dubs as they were called, to a few record companies. Mercury Records rejected them. Several other local companies rejected them.

I went to New York, using some of the money I had earned working for my father, and after several days of rejections left New York for Chicago, where I decided to investigate the black record companies.

I called one of them, Apex Records, and spoke to a Dempsey Nelson, the president of the company. Nelson invited me to stop by and play it for his producer. Apex Records was located on the south side of Chicago. After entering a small storefront entrance I was greeted by a receptionist, who brought me to a small waiting room outfitted with rather old beat-up furniture.

I waited for about an hour. The producer for the company greeted me and took me into a rather barren room with just a record player and speakers and played my Santa song. After a few seconds, he flipped it over and listened to "Is it Chilly in Chile during Christmas?" A few seconds later he said, "I'm afraid ya ain't going to make it with that stuff. What else ya got?"

I then gave him my "Mudder Goose" dub and he played it. After each rhyme, he laughed loudly and listened to the whole tune. He then said, "Wow, good friend, you've got a smash."

He quickly ushered me into the president's office. Dempsey Nelson was a large man with a mustache who chomped a cigar and smiled simultaneously. The producer told him, "We've got a stone smash single, Dempsey. Don't let this guy leave 'til we sign him up."

Dempsey heard my dub, laughed louder than the producer and convinced me to sign up with him. "I'll call RCA records, rent their largest recording studio," he said, "and you'll be on the air in a few weeks."

Here I was on the way to stardom. So of course I signed the contract. "Could you write a few more songs," Dempsey urged. The session would require four songs.

"Yes, I will," I assured him and off I went. I contacted Dick and we worked out a few more songs for the session, such immortal songs as "Flip-flop Fanny," for example. I can't remember the other two, but they definitely weren't classics.

Dick would accompany me on the piano and would attend the session and get paid musician's scale for his effort. Meanwhile, Nelson hired four backup singers and an entire band and we were all set for the big evening session at RCA Studio A. What a thrill. Look what I had created. All these people here because of me.

At the session, the group played the songs, the backup singers accompanied me and there I was, hearing my songs for the first time—and, boy, did they sound great. Everybody was patting me on the back: "Joe, you've got a stone smash hit."

To say that I was thrilled was putting it mildly. Dreams of fame, of beautiful women begging me for my autograph, of national publicity as my novelty tune hit the top of charts—all this raced through my mind during those few days after the session.

As a recording artist, I also changed my name to something better fitting the image of the song. I called myself Joe Subway.

With fame assured, I gave serious thought to quitting school for a semester so I could tour the country and make personal appearances. I found it difficult to go back to work for my father to be a delivery boy and do other odd jobs. The excitement and expectations kept me on a high for over two weeks.

But for some strange reason I hadn't heard from Dempsey. So I called him. "How's it going?" I asked.

"Not too good, Joe. Could I see you?" he said in a rather concerned and serious way.

"What's wrong?" I asked.

"Just come down and I'll explain," he said.

I arrived at his office and was told to take a seat in his

reception room. All sorts of horrible things passed through my mind. Dempsey kept me waiting for two hours before I was escorted into his office.

"We've got a few financial problems," said Dempsey. "That last record we had didn't take off as we had expected. We're very short on funds, and to be frank, Joe, we don't have the money to pay for the sound mixing and the records to get this thing kicked off."

"How much will it take?" I asked.

"About $1,500 to get to the record stage," he replied as he shrugged his shoulders.

"If I raise the money to get the records pressed, could I put the record on my own label and work out a joint venture with you?"

"Sure," said Dempsey. "What label have you got?"

"I don't have any yet, but give me a few days and I'll get one," I answered.

I saw this whole turn of events as a great opportunity to start my own record company. Not only would I have my own song, but I would own half the company as well. Dempsey had agreed to pay me back half of everything I spent to get that record pressed, and I felt I couldn't lose.

I managed to convince my father to loan me $1,500 and I proceeded to get the MAD record label for my very own. In about three weeks I had pressed over a thousand records and was now well on my way to stardom. I dropped off a few hundred records with Dempsey and told him that he could "do his thing"—get that record on the radio.

Dempsey, however, called me a week later and told me that before anybody would play it, there had to be some publicity and advertisements in *Billboard* and *Cashbox* magazines. No problem, I thought. With such a smash hit, I wasn't going to let a few advertisements get in the way, so I contacted some advertising people and created a series of three advertisements, which I gave Dempsey to run in the various magazines.

Meanwhile, I called Richard—a local disc jockey who owned a

record store on the south side—and offered to give him some free records if he would play the tune. I sent out mailings to radio stations all over the country. I sent letters to disc jockeys and I tried to get Dempsey to run those advertisements in the magazines. But I couldn't seem to reach him.

Nothing worked. We did sell a few records in Richard's record store, but the mailing didn't work, the disc jockey mailing produced nothing, and Dempsey Nelson literally disappeared. His storefront business closed and his creditors were now after me to pay all his other bills—none of which was ever mine in the first place.

My dreams of becoming a great songwriter, a star performer—even a record company owner—slowly crumbled around me. I was in debt to my father for about $3,000 and figured that I'd just be able to pay him off if I could work the rest of the summer and the next Christmas break. I did.

I still had about five hundred records left but, unfortunately, nobody was interested in Joe Subway's latest smash single. Not even my father.

4
Miami's Loss, the Army's Gain

It was now my last year of college. My grades were excellent, I was active in extracurricular activities and I was even enjoying ROTC (Reserve Officer Training Corps). For some reason I liked the military and ROTC gave me the opportunity to go into the army as an officer. It didn't work out that way, however. After spending three and a half years in school, I received my draft notice.

I took the notice and returned it to my local draft board, advising them that I was a student at the university's engineering school and that I was in ROTC and needed just one more semester to graduate and also become an army officer.

The draft board had different ideas. It would not grant me a deferment. I had violated one of its regulations by not reporting my school status, and despite my good grades, my ROTC status, and my appeals, they refused to defer me for one more semester.

The Berlin Wall had gone up and the draft quotas were taking quantum leaps. They needed me to fill their quotas and there was nothing I could do to change their minds. The army ironically lost an officer and the world lost another electrical engineer.

So off I went to Fort Carson, Colorado, for basic training. When I arrived at the camp, I took a series of tests along with the rest of the troops. Coming right out of college, I scored almost 100 percent on everything. After about six weeks of basic training, I was called to attend a special meeting conducted by some men wearing civilian clothes. There were three soldiers with me at the meeting, which started out like a scene from a stereotyped war movie.

"We called you men out of the company because of those high scores you got on your tests. We've got a special mission for you if you'll accept it. If not, no problem; you can go back to your squads."

The special mission was two years as intelligence agents in Germany. We would be sent to a special spy school in Baltimore, Maryland, and then shipped off to Germany for a year of intensive German language training.

The deal sounded great to me—anything was better than playing soldier—and one of the benefits of the program was that I would wear civilian clothes and live among the German people. And, if I was lucky, even meet a few of those gorgeous German women. But there was one catch. Instead of putting in two years, I would have to enlist for three. I enlisted for three.

I went to Fort Holabird, the special spy school, and then went to Germany where I learned German in one year. It was hard, intensive training but after I finished, I spoke it almost flaw-lessly. Because of my electrical engineering background, I was assigned to the army's surveillance attachment. When we were not planting bugs and listening devices, we were looking for them. My work took me all over Germany and through some very interesting experiences.

Halfway through my active army career, I occasionally was assigned to the CIA to look after Russian defectors. They were usually low-level army defectors who were in the process of being debriefed by the CIA, and it was my job to keep them out of trouble.

The defectors would get an allowance and freedom to move about Frankfurt as long as I guarded them. And where did they go every night? Down to Kaiserstrasse, Frankfurt's red-light district, to watch all the strip shows and blow their allowances.

I knew every stripper, every B-girl, and every bit of gossip on the street. When one of my buddies would land in Frankfurt and want to see the strip shows, I'd take him to a few and the girls would rush up to me as if I owned the place to see who my new big-spending guest would be.

After my three years with the army, I was discharged in Europe. I went to visit some of my father's European business associates, who were interested in having me help them open up a ski-lift sales organization in the United States.

I was given a two-week tour of the Austrian Alps and their ski resorts with my own personal ski teacher. I also invited an engineering friend from Miami to take the tour with me. After my tour I returned to Frankfurt to get my things packed and think over the ski deal. I arrived at a small Frankfurt hotel and accidentally bumped into the Russian ambassador at the registration desk. The hotel was located near the American Embassy and the Russians would often stay close to the American facility.

I dropped into the hotel totally unexpectedly, so the chance meeting could not have been preplanned. Realizing the valuable intelligence contact I had just accidentally made, and with three solid years of intelligence experience and training, I knew exactly what to do to make the Russian think that I was willing to get him all sorts of valuable information for a price.

He thought he really had a hot source. Little did he know. I contacted my friends at the CIA and worked under strict cover until things got too hot for me and I left Germany after a few months of high-level activity. I learned later that my chance contact turned into a very valuable operation for the CIA and my replacement managed to carry on nicely after I left.

Back in the States, I held two jobs. One was with my father, helping him with advertising, and the second was organizing the newly formed ski-lift company with the help of my friend. I was twenty-seven in 1965 when I set up Ski-Lift International.

5
Batman and Robin

During my first year with SLI (Ski-Lift International), with the help of artists and designers, I created sales literature, brochures, magazine advertisements, and direct mail promotions. The material was so professional that we looked like a real contender in the ski-lift industry in which we had nine competitors.

Sam Bonasso, my engineering school classmate and new partner, was one of those hail-fellow-well-met types who always had a smile on his cherubic face and knew how to charm people. He was in charge of sales and engineering and once I developed a hot lead, he'd follow it up for the final sale.

But I was too blunt to satisfy our Swiss and Austrian owners. While I was in charge, they would try to overload us with inventory or tell us how to run things and I was very quick to point out my dissatisfaction.

They could convince Sam of their ideas, but they couldn't

convince me. I only had a 10 percent interest in the company—
the same as Sam—and although I did not have control of the
company, I did call the shots in the United States.

On a few occasions when we sold a ski-lift, the resort that
purchased one was so impressed with our promotion and advertising that they asked me to help them with their advertising.
Before long I had two ski resorts for clients, and among SLI, my
ski resort clients, and my father's business, I decided to form my
own advertising agency to capitalize on the 15 percent advertising commission normally given agencies by the media.

SLI was profitable and held a very visible position in the
industry within one year. I was quite proud of the job I had
done, and so was Sam. But the Europeans were not. I was a
thorn in their side, a pain in the neck who didn't give them the
freedom they wanted to control our company from abroad. In
addition, they tried to get us to hire the Austrian inventor's
brother-in-law. I disapproved. Finally, after one and a half
years, they met with Sam and me and asked me to resign.

They appointed Sam the new president and asked if I would
continue handling some of the advertising. Sam took over and I
helped him a little with the advertising but decided later to drop
the account entirely and sell my stock back to the group.

Sam did well for a short while but floundered and control was
then passed to the Austrian inventor's brother-in-law. He practically drove the company into the ground. SLI went bankrupt a
few years after that, with a several-million-dollar loss. I took no
great pleasure in the news. I'm sorry to see anybody lose like
they did, but it was their company and their folly, and it gave
me the confidence that maybe I really did know what I was
doing.

Out of this episode I formed my own advertising agency. At
the time I had four accounts, a secretary, and an office at my
father's factory on the south side of Chicago. His company was
then called Consolidated International.

My accounts included Bryces Mountain Resort in Bayse,
Virginia; Schuss Mountain in Mancelona, Michigan; and an

assortment of small restaurants. I used outside artists and typesetting, and I would write the copy.

In early 1966 the Batman fad swept the nation. And if you remember it, you'll also remember that whatever product had the Batman name on it sold like hot cakes. There were Batman T-shirts, Batman toys, Batman combs, even a Batman peanut butter—you name a product and there was a similar product with the name Batman on it. Around the same time, credit cards were also a big fad. Bank Americard and Master Charge had just announced their programs. American Express and Diners Club were growing rapidly.

I had a wild idea right at the very start of the Batman craze. Why not produce a Batman credit card—a plastic card embossed with a person's name and a special personal number? The cards would resemble a real credit card in size, shape, and thickness. A Batman credit card, however, would have no value. It was really just a satire on the new credit card explosion.

My idea involved advertising the card on radio stations throughout the country and selling them for one dollar, with the owners' names embossed on the cards. For every card we'd sell, we would also capture that person's name on a mailing list. With the mailing list we could send out a Batman catalog, conduct contests, and really tie the whole fad nicely together.

I called up the Licensing Corporation of America, the group that was licensing the rights to Batman, and finally, after several calls, I got through to Murray Altschuler, one of their representatives.

I told Murray that I had an idea for a new Batman product that could be the hottest selling item in their entire line. Murray replied, "Joe, we've already got Batman T-shirts, Batman toys, Batman shoes—what could you have that's different? Everything possible is now licensed and on my list."

I said, "Well, I've got a Batman credit card." There was silence. It was as if Murray were looking up and down his list, unable to find a Batman credit card.

"That's certainly different," he said. "Tell me about it." I proceeded to tell him about my idea, the catalog, the mailing list, and my marketing approach. Murray thought it sounded so good that he asked me to come quickly to New York with my plan. He wanted to present it to the principals of LCA.

I flew to New York with my presentation. I had drawings of the card, mock-ups of the mailing packages, and radio scripts for the spot commercials. Despite the few days it took me to put it together, it looked good, and I was totally prepared.

I arrived in New York, walked into LCA's office and waited to see Murray. I noticed how busy the phone lines were and how quickly people were moving. It was really a madhouse—something you could imagine from the way the Batman fad was taking off.

After I had been waiting an hour, Murray brought me into his office and I made my presentation. When I was finished Murray picked up a phone and called in Allan Stone and Jay Emmett, the two principals of LCA. "I've got something you've got to see," he said calmly. "It's very important. Hold all your calls."

After my presentation to the group, all they could do was shake their heads and smile. "Fantastic idea," said Stone. "Would you entertain a partnership or joint venture to really launch your concept?"

The idea appealed to me. Rather than be selfish and hog the whole deal for myself, by sharing it with them I'd have an advantage no other licensee would have. I'd have their full cooperation on making my program a success. And then if any future deals came up, I'd have first shot.

It took me about four seconds to accept. "It's a deal," I said, shaking their hands.

"Go back to Chicago and get those cards printed," said Emmett. "This fad hasn't peaked yet and we don't want to be too late."

They suggested I print a quarter of a million of them for the first run and get my lawyers to draw up the corporate papers. We were to split everything on a fifty-fifty basis, and they agreed to put up half the money so there was less risk on my part.

I flew back to Chicago dreaming of the millions I was going to make, of my new Playboy mansion, and of that chauffeur-driven Cadillac limousine I was going to buy. I even took time out to plan the big effort I was going to make to launch my new company.

The first thing I did was contact my attorney, Maurice Raizes, and get him started on the contract. Then I went to the credit card printer.

I picked the best credit card printer in Chicago—the one that all the banks were using to print their credit cards.

When I arrived, I was met by the chief credit card salesman for the company. I introduced myself as being from my advertising agency and he took me for a tour of the facility, where I saw huge presses churning out all sorts of plastic cards. There was plenty of security, and at every entrance armed guards stood by, making sure nobody walked off with the plastic money they were printing. In a way, it was like touring a mint.

We then sat together in the salesman's office to discuss my big project. "I'll need a quarter of a million credit cards," I said.

"For what bank?" he asked.

"Not a bank," I replied, "but for a major national account— Batman."

"Batman?" he asked, rather puzzled.

"Yes, we need a quarter of a million Batman credit cards by next week," I said. I then explained my idea, how I had called Murray and then flown to New York. I described how LCA had fallen in love with the idea and become my new partner. I told him how vital it was that I get the cards as quickly as possible, because we did not know the duration of the fad and we wanted to capture Batman's momentum before it peaked. "How soon can we get a quarter million Batman credit cards?"

The salesman looked at me and shook his head. "The best I can do is eight weeks."

"Eight weeks? That's no good. It's got to be this week or we may miss the fad. Why eight weeks?" I asked.

"You have to wait two weeks for plates," he replied. "And then we have a dozen customers waiting to get on press. That alone will take six weeks."

I couldn't believe that my big dream was about to crumble because I couldn't get on press. "Could I have the name of your plate-makers? Maybe I can get a plate faster if I explain my problem."

"Sure" said the salesman, "all the power to you. If you can get the plates sooner, I still can't help you because I've got so many customers waiting in line."

There had to be a way. I couldn't let this opportunity pass. "What if I took the names of your customers and convinced them all to let me get in front of them? I'm sure they'll appreciate and understand the urgency of what I'm doing."

"Joe, if you can do it, be my guest." And with that he pulled out eight files from his drawer and proceeded to read off the names and phone numbers of several of his customers.

Without wasting any time, I drove straight to the plate-maker in downtown Chicago and spent an hour trying to convince him of the importance of the job. I finally got a commitment from him that he'd have the plates for me in two days.

Returning to my office, I called all the names the salesman gave me and got enough of his customers to let me step ahead of them so that I was assured of getting on press within the week.

One of my calls was to the First National Bank of Chicago. They not only let me step ahead of them, but they offered to put their Data Processing Department at my disposal.

We worked out a deal whereby the First National Bank would receive the orders, deposit the checks or cash, and then produce a magnetic tape that could be used by the embossing company to emboss the credit cards and also by the company that would later mail out the cards.

I also got Addressograph Multigraph Corporation to commit to embossing the cards and a large Chicago mailer to mail them out.

Meanwhile I had sent out the corporate contracts to LCA and was waiting for their licensing contract.

Within one week after I returned from New York, the credit cards started coming off the presses and I started storing them in my office. I conducted a few tests with adults who were unaware of my involvement with the program and was offered $5 for an unembossed card—a card we were going to sell for $1. If you remember the fad, the demand for Batman products was so great that companies couldn't produce them fast enough. And I had the first really unusual Batman product—one that appealed to adults as well as to teens and children.

I produced my radio spots at WCFL, a local Chicago radio station. Dick Orkin, one of the station's creative talents, had just started a radio series called Chickenman, which was a spoof of Batman, and his series was being aired daily on WCFL. I had him do the spots for me and placed a schedule on the radio station to start at about the time the credit cards were supposed to be completed. The six spots were humorous satires on the whole credit card scene and cost me over $1,000. Today Dick Orkin's expertise costs $50,000 and he's one of radio's most successful talents and, I'm proud to say, a good friend of mine.

I called an old friend from my Army Intelligence days, Greg O'Bierne. He was in between jobs but agreed to join me in my venture and bring his wife and child with him to Chicago to live. He moved almost as quickly as I did, and he had an apartment and his belongings in Chicago within a week.

I had everything covered. I had the printing, promotion, fulfillment, help, and was even working on some future projects when I realized that I still had not received the contracts and the license to sell my Batman credit cards. The radio schedule was all set to run and everybody was primed and ready to roll, but I didn't want to give the station the approval to run the spots without a contract.

So I called Murray. He was busy, so I left a message. Still no word from Murray so I called again. He was still busy so I started getting concerned. The radio station was calling me and my room was filling up with Batman credit cards. A quarter of a million Batman credit cards, incidentally, would take up an entire ten-foot-by-twelve-foot room—that's a lot of credit cards.

It was obvious after two days of calling Murray and his two associates, and not getting a call back, that something was wrong. I quickly flew to New York, went to their office and waited in the reception room for two hours—just to see Murray.

Murray finally walked into the reception room looking very sheepish. "Joe," he said as he cleared his throat, "I don't know how to tell you this, but we couldn't get your license approved. All licenses must be approved by Mr. Liebowitz, the chairman of the board of National Periodical Publications, owner of the Batman rights. And Mr. Liebowitz didn't like your idea and refused to sign the contract."

I wasn't daunted. I had been told it took eight weeks to get on press, and we had our cards in a week. Now my challenge was to convince the only person left who could stop me. So I had Murray call Mr. Liebowitz so I could meet with him personally.

Mr. Liebowitz was a short pudgy man who sat behind a large, clean, polished desk. As I walked into his office he pressed an intercom button to page his secretary. "Marie, get me a cigar," he said.

I expected to see Marie walk in with a cigar but instead she walked up to the edge of his desk, opened a small wooden box on his desk, pulled out a cigar, unwrapped it and put it in his mouth and lit it. When I saw that, I knew I was in trouble.

"Go ahead kid, what's on your mind?" he said.

I proceeded to explain the history of the program. I explained how I had a quarter of a million Batman credit cards sitting in my office. I told him how I had my entire savings in the project and that I owed thousands of dollars to my suppliers. I asked for his understanding and mercy. Then he finally spoke: "I don't like it. I've made $60 million already with this Batman thing and I've made enough. I'm afraid people might think your Batman credit card is a real one and I don't want to be sued. Besides I don't like it. Period."

I pleaded with him to let me sell just enough to pay my bills, thinking that the promotion would be so successful that he wouldn't want to stop me. He refused to budge an inch and stuck to his decision. I even threatened a lawsuit and he replied, "Not against me. Take it up with your partners at LCA."

And my partners at LCA were no help either. "Sorry, Joe, you did it without a license. It's your tough luck; we can't help you," said Murray.

There was nothing I could do or say. It's one thing to realize that you have lost an opportunity to make a million, but it's another thing to realize that you are now broke and owe people money.

Here, I had the opportunity of a lifetime snatched from my grasp. I was planning on making millions. I was studying Cadillac brochures, reading the real estate sections of the newspapers, dreaming of my new mansion—and suddenly it all collapsed. It was almost too hard to believe.

I returned to Chicago and promptly canceled the radio spots. Then I totaled all my expenses. Aside from what I owed I had two other problems. First, I had no idea what Greg could do at this point. Second, I had no idea what to do with a quarter of a million Batman credit cards.

The Batman experience was a very traumatic one for me. If I ever had to list my biggest disappointment, it had to be my Batman experience.

I didn't give up, however. I moved the Batman credit cards to a warehouse and stored them there. If I had owned Batman T-shirts, I probably could have sold them in some other country or offered them to some ravage-torn disaster area. But I had Batman credit cards—useless pieces of plastic with no intrinsic value. There was nothing I could do with them short of burying them or holding on to them.

I tried to keep Greg busy in my advertising agency, but we both realized that the handwriting was on the wall. I was thousands of dollars in debt and there was little that Greg could do to help me at that time so he packed his belongings, his wife and child, and returned to Philadelphia.

I struggled through the next few years convincing my

suppliers that I would pay them back. Finally, after two long hard years, I paid my last bill and decided that very day I'd give my old friend Murray Altschuler a call. "Murray, this is Joe Sugarman," I said.

"Joe Sugarman, Joe Sugarman . . ." said Murray.

"Remember," I said, "the Batman credit card?"

"Joe Sugarman, sure, the Batman credit card. How are you?"

"Fine, Murray," I said. "You know I still have a quarter of a million Batman credit cards and the thought occurred to me that maybe I could get my license now. The Batman fad is dead and I thought maybe my efforts could get things rolling again."

"Joe, it's funny you called," replied Murray. "LCA was just acquired by National Periodical Publications and now that we're all one team, you may have a chance. Let me check out the idea and call you back."

It wasn't long before Murray called me back. "Sorry, Joe, but the answer is still no. Mr. Liebowitz still doesn't like your idea. Maybe some other time."

A few more years went by and I called Murray again. I had just moved the credit cards to a new location and I was curious to see if Murray was still around. The switchboard operator connected me to a young lady who said, "Mr. Altschuler's office." Evidently Murray now had a personal secretary.

When Murray finally answered, it didn't take him too long to recognize me. "Murray," I said, "this is Joe Sugarman."

"Joe," was the reply. "How are you?"

"Fine," I said. "I was wondering if you would consider resubmitting my Batman credit card for a license? I still have a quarter of a million of them."

"Joe, it's funny you called," he said. "National Periodical Publications has a new president. He's Jay Emmett. Do you remember him?"

What a break, I thought. Here was the same guy who loved my idea back when I first presented it and now he was in charge of the company that owns the Batman rights.

"Of course," I replied. "I remember him well. See if he'll go for me trying at least a test to see if I can sell the card. The fad has been dead for years. I can really accomplish something if I can get it going."

It didn't take Murray longer than a few days to call me back. "Sorry, Joe, I checked with Jay and he told me to take a pass on the deal. He's new as president and doesn't want to make a move for a while that would upset Mr. Liebowitz. Call me in a few years."

About three years later I called Murray again. It was now 1976, I had my own mail order business, and I had achieved a high degree of visibility and success.

"Murray," I said, "I thought I'd give you a call again to see if there was a possibility of having you license my Batman credit cards. I still have a quarter of a million of them."

"Joe, it's funny you called," Murray said. "National Periodical Publications was just bought out by Warner Communications and I'm sure they'll be interested. Warner is really promotion-minded and I think we'll have a chance."

Murray called back a few days later. "Joe, they rejected the idea. They're too early in the merger for a deal like this. I would suggest calling back once they get their feet on the ground."

It was in early 1978 that I called Murray back. Warner Communications was working on its $40 million Superman movie that was scheduled for release at the end of the year.

Batman was still running on TV, both as a cartoon show and in reruns from the 1966 show. It was now twelve years later and it appeared that Batman was actually going through a slight revival.

I now felt better about my chances than ever before. So did Murray when I called him in February.

"Joe, it's funny you called," said Murray quite optimistically. "Warner Communications is really promotion-minded now—especially with their Superman movie coming out this year. Maybe there's a chance. Let me call you back."

And so I waited, and a few days later I received a call from Murray. "Joe, I don't know how to tell you this, but they've accepted your license and I want you to come to New York so we can draw up the papers."

What a thrill! After waiting twelve years to get the license, I finally got it. What a tremendous feeling of accomplishment I had. And then I thought that maybe it was fate. Here I was with twelve years of experience in mail order—better qualified to handle the promotion than ever before. Finally I had the opportunity I had worked twelve years to get. "Murray," I shouted, "I'm so thrilled, I can't begin to tell you how I feel."

And Murray, who sounded as thrilled as I was, said "Joe, I have never felt as good about issuing a license in my life as I feel about the license I'm about to issue you. Congratulations!"

"Murray," I said, "I'm not going to disappoint you. I'm going to write the best damn mail order ad of my life. You'll be proud as hell, Murray, I promise you."

So I flew to New York, had a celebration luncheon with Murray and some of the principals of Warner Communications, and received a contract, which I promptly sent to the same lawyer who drew up the original corporate papers twelve years earlier.

Maurice Raizes, my lawyer, looked over the contract and approved it. The contract gave me the rights to conduct a test campaign for which I was under no obligation. If the test proved successful, I would pay them $25,000 as a guarantee against a certain percentage of the sales of the cards.

Here, after being in my own mail order business for almost seven years, with all my experience, I now had the opportunity to run an ad that meant more to me than any other advertisement I had ever written.

I worked on my Batman mail order ad for two solid weeks. I was determined to make it the finest ad I had ever written. And indeed it was. After I finished it, I was proud. It was the type of ad that I knew would work.

So I ran the advertisement in the southwestern edition of the *Wall Street Journal*, where we test all of our advertising. From this test I have always been able to determine exactly how many items I could sell through hundreds of other national magazines and newspapers.

Instead of selling the card for $1, my price was now $5. Inflation had taken its toll. And instead of using radio commercials, I was using magazine and newspaper advertisements.

The ad needed only two hundred responses to break even, and I was so confident I geared up for over one thousand responses. When the ad finally ran, my response was only twelve.

The ad failed miserably. I had tried and failed for twelve straight years only to fail once and for all.

I wrote Murray, thanked him for his help and advice, and for sharing the joy of issuing the contract. I told him of the dismal results and gave him my best wishes for his new Superman movie.

I still have a quarter of a million Batman credit cards. They really are neat. Each card has "Batman Credit Card" on the front with room to emboss your name and humorous terms and conditions on the back. There's also a special signature panel on the back to make it look really authentic.

I recently offered them for $5. However, for readers of this book, I'll be happy to send you a blank unembossed free sample if you'll kindly send me $1 for handling and a self-addressed stamped envelope to "Credit Card," One JS&A Plaza, Northbrook, Illinois 60062.

6
The Great
Teeny Bopper Society

In 1966, when I first discovered I had a quarter of a million Batman credit cards and no license to sell them, I was really crushed. My dreams shattered, I realized I had to pick myself up and start over.

One of the first things I did when I realized my plight was to get some publicity with the hope that somebody might be able to help. I called up the *Chicago Tribune* advertising editor and told him about my problem. He laughed and decided to do a story.

The story started out, "Can anyone help Joe Sugarman?" and told the tale of my Batman adventure.

The article drew a number of letters and even dollar bills for the credit cards and a strange call from a Mr. Frank Camp.

"Mr. Sugarman, I read about your story in the *Chicago Tribune* and I think maybe you can help me," he said in a slow, raspy deep voice. "I've got a quarter of a million Twist'n Pops sitting in my warehouse and I thought you might be just the guy to help me get rid of them."

So I went to Camp's warehouse and saw what a Twist'n Pop was. It was a plastic paddle ball game about two feet long with two big paddles separated by a plastic rod. A ball on a string was tied to the middle. The object of the game was to bounce the ball from paddle to paddle. It was easy to master, and once you got the ball moving it looked as if you were doing the twist—a dance rage of the early sixties.

But here we were in 1966. The twist was dead and along with it the Twist'n Pop. Like Joe Sugarman, Frank Camp was the victim of some major miscalculation. And ironically, by the same number.

Seeing Camp's predicament didn't make me feel too bad. A quarter of a million Twist'n Pops took up an entire 50,000-square-foot warehouse. The cartons were stacked ceiling high and everywhere you looked there were Twist'n Pops—in his office, in the locker room, and on top of the loading dock. Only in the narrow aisles and around a few machines were there open spaces where Camp stacked small wire garden fences he manufactured for Sears.

"You sound like you might be good at promotion," commented Camp. "Why don't you work out a program? I'll supply the Twist'n Pops, you supply the promotion, and we'll share the profits."

If there were ever two losers, they were Frank and me. And I certainly understood his predicament. He seemed like an honest guy who had obviously made a mistake.

So I accepted the challenge. The deal was simple. I would put up $10,000 worth of my time and promotion money and Frank would give me 10,000 Twist'n Pops in return. After I sold my 10,000 pieces, I would then start to sell his product and share the profits.

The first thing I did was change the name. The dance called the twist had been dead for several years, but a new term was now part of the nation's vocabulary—teeny bopper, the new name for the music-loving teens of the late sixties. Lyndon

Johnson was president and his "Great Society" program was the nation's new buzz word.

So I renamed the product the Teeny Bopper and I decided to form a club—the Great Teeny Bopper Society. I got a popular WCFL disc jockey, Ron Britain, to work with me on a radio promotion for his show.

The idea was exciting. Members would join the club by sending a self-addressed stamped envelope to the station. In return they would get a membership card, button, and bumper sticker. Hopefully, this would create the first wave of a fad that would eventually help sell our warehouse full of Teeny Boppers. All we would have to do is announce the Teeny Boppers' availability on spot radio commercials and everybody would rush to the store and pick one up.

I had 20,000 membership kits printed up. I still owed money from my Batman fiasco, but I was convinced that this promotion would be a huge success and worth the gamble.

Then I had my next-door neighbor, Sam Bird, read the Great Teeny Bopper Society pledge. Sam was ninety years old and sounded every year of it. He loved the idea and recorded the pledge on my small tape recorder. We played the pledge every day on the air, and hearing the Great Teeny Bopper pledge being read by a ninety-year-old man was the talk of the station.

Then I would take the tape recorder and record other people. The mailman would come to my door and I'd give him a script to read: "My name is Sam Konitz and I'm a mailman. I'm also a proud member of Ron Britain's Great Teeny Bopper Society."

I got over fifty people to read something similar. I got our butcher, my lawyer, several people at a nursing home—anyone over fifty years old qualified perfectly for my recording sessions.

When the responses came in, they poured in. Ron Britain would play the tapes on the air and then urge his audience to send for the kits and join the Great Teeny Bopper Society. I had my whole family helping me stuff envelopes. Letters came in from all over the Midwest—from doctors and lawyers as well as teenagers.

I then selected a chain of discount stores throughout Chicago to stock the Teeny Boppers and contracted for a series of radio commercials announcing the Teeny Boppers' availability at those local stores. With 20,000 members of the Great Teeny Bopper Society I would be able to launch the product, and if Chicago proved a good test market, I could launch the campaign nationally.

Meanwhile, I had received a call from Bruce Gilbert of the Coca-Cola Company in Atlanta. I had sent them information on the Great Teeny Bopper Society on the hunch that if I could tie in with them and have them sponsor the program nationally, we'd have a huge success. They were interested and asked that I fly to Atlanta and present the concept to them.

Before I left I stuffed two big suitcases with the responses we had been getting from our promotion. The envelopes were already filled with the membership materials, so I figured I'd mail them from the Atlanta airport before I returned. I wanted them with me in case Coca-Cola wanted to see the responses we were actually getting.

I arrived in Atlanta, went straight to Coca-Cola's main office on Peachtree Street, and made my presentation to Gilbert and his staff. It went well and then they popped the question, "What kind of response did you get?"

I told them to see for themselves, and on their big conference room table I poured out the two large suitcases. A heap of mail stared them in the eyes. They started sorting through the letters—three nuns from Indianapolis, Xerox Corporation, General Motors. The return envelopes looked so impressive that they were going through them like kids in a candy factory.

I packed my suitcases and left with the feeling that they were genuinely impressed. I even left with a few recordings of their voices saying things like "I'm Ralph Pinzer. I'm a brain surgeon and I'm a proud member of the Great Teeny Bopper Society." They, too, were joining in on the craziness.

They were to call me with a decision shortly after my big Teeny Bopper promotion, which was coming up the following week. The radio commercials were being aired as I returned to Chicago. I had already filled the stores with Teeny Boppers and

I was gambling a thousand dollars of my own money to pay for the radio spots.

I had selected one of Community Discount's larger stores as the key introductory store, and I had hired models to demonstrate my Teeny Boppers. Who were the models? The Grandmothers Club of Chicago. I couldn't think of a more appropriate group.

I also hired Ron Britain to make a personal appearance, hired a rock band, and planned for a real gala event.

I was really taking a chance. I had lost a fortune with my Batman promotion and I was still paying it off. I had to do well with the Teeny Bopper program or I was going to have one awful time surviving.

But I wasn't worried at all. The promotion was going so well that I couldn't help but succeed. I had a big potential program with Coca-Cola and it looked like clear sailing in Chicago. I had no product to manufacture, and if the thing took off, I had a great chance to make that million dollars I missed making with the Batman promotion.

I just knew the promotion was going to be a huge success. It was April, the weather had been warm, and the Teeny Bopper would make a great spring product. The radio station was being inundated with calls from people reconfirming the time and place of the big unveiling. The discount stores had received so many calls that they moved the planned location of the Teeny Boppers to the entrance. I couldn't ask for better cooperation.

Everything was in place that Friday. I had scheduled the introduction for two o'clock in the afternoon, and each hour of the day leading up to that time I checked off what had to be done. I absolutely was not going to let one detail slip through my fingers. This time I wasn't going to be stopped by the lack of someone's approval as I had been with the Batman credit card. I was confident that nothing short of an act of God was going to stop me from making it this time.

A few hours before my scheduled grand opening, a tornado struck the Chicago area, killing several people and wiping out my promotion. It was the blow that I didn't expect—the act of

God that proved fatal for the entire program. I couldn't re-schedule the campaign because I was broke. I had lost all the money on the radio spots, the band I had hired, and myriad other expenses. And once I lost the momentum, that was it.

In addition, Coca-Cola called me the following week to advise me that they were removing their interest in the program. *Time* magazine had mentioned in an article that Teeny Bopper was the name associated with dope-swallowing teenagers, and Coca-Cola didn't want to hurt their image.

Within just a few years I had been struck by more disappointments than most people could take in a lifetime. Two major promotions had success written all over them and yet they totally collapsed in sudden and unexpected crashes.

But I did not give up. As long as I could feed myself and pay back my debts, I would continue. I simply took most of my 10,000 Teeny Boppers and put them next to my quarter of a million Batman credit cards and carried on.

During the Batman episode I met Wendy, an English girl. I dated her during the Teeny Bopper promotion and finally moved out of my parents' home in Oak Park to be closer to her on Chicago's North Shore.

I had my own apartment to pay for and I also moved my office from my father's factory and put it into my apartment. My father had walked out on my mother and asked for a divorce to marry his secretary of twenty years. My mom took it kind of hard and I didn't like the rather cold way my father walked out on her. I just thought that it wasn't fair and didn't want any part of him. I stopped doing advertising for him, and I stopped talking to him for a while.

I tried to give my mother some support and help during this time, but things were so hectic that I didn't provide enough. She had a nervous breakdown and was in pretty bad shape for more than a year, but with the help of my three younger sisters we managed to pull her through.

I'm friends with my father now, but it took a long time to heal the wounds.

7
Teen Club Promoter

During my Teeny Bopper promotion, I needed a band to entertain at my grand opening. I heard a group called the Maybees playing in a nearby suburban bar. Wendy and I had stopped in to go dancing one evening and really enjoyed their music. When I needed a group to perform for me, I thought of the Maybees and went back to the bar where I had first seen them. But they were gone. The manager told me that they were now playing as a regular group at Frank Bond's Teen Club on Harlem Avenue in Berwyn, a western suburb.

I went over there one evening and met Frank Bond—a Damon Runyon-type character who owned a restaurant and bar and a large banquet room. Bond would rent out the banquet room on Friday nights to a local promoter who would stage live rock bands for the kids in the area. The promoter would book the rock groups, charge for admission, and pay all the expenses. What was left was split between Bond and the promoter.

When I stepped into his bar, I found him sitting at a table eating dinner with his girlfriend. Bond was about fifty years old and reminded me of a stereotyped Chicago gangster from the early twenties.

"Sit down," he grunted. "What can I do for ya?"

I introduced myself and told him that I was staging a big promotion and needed a rock group. I told him about the Teeny Bopper, how we had had a big campaign on WCFL, and how I had heard the Maybees at another bar and tracked them down to his place. I explained that I wanted to hire them for my big promotion.

Bond just listened as I explained, and after I finished he paused for a minute, chewed his food, and then said, "How would you like to promote this place? The guy who's doin' it now isn't worth a damn. I end up running the dances myself.

"All you do is book the group, hire a disc jockey, and sell tickets at the door. Then at ten o'clock ya kick the kids out, pay the group, pay $100 for the rental of the room, and we split the profits. Ya can't beat that. It's a smooth deal."

I accepted the challenge, but on the condition that it wait until my Teeny Bopper promotion finished the following week. And as you know, it indeed was finished the following week.

Frank Bond couldn't have come at a better time. Broke, with just barely enough to pay rent and eat, I needed the extra work. It was at night, too, which meant it left my days free to do my advertising.

Frank Bond's Club was fun, too. It was there I really learned the art of promotion. Whenever I would try to hype a big dance, it would flop. Whenever I presented the dance honestly, the kids responded. And I never really knew for sure which dance would be big and which dance would be a bomb. There was always the element of surprise.

Wendy took tickets at the entrance and I was the MC on stage. I tried different promotions. During one dance I called for a battle of the bands. Normally, groups battle each other by playing their music, with the audience voting for the best group.

My battle was different. I had both groups put down their instruments, put on boxing gloves, and battle it out on stage. It usually drew a big crowd and occasionally a little blood—but the kids loved it.

I'd hold dance contests with no music, and if you ever wanted to see a strange sight, that was it—squirming, gyrating teens moving to no sound.

On special occasions I'd offer unusual prizes like Joe Subway records, Teeny Boppers, Batman credit cards, and even a round trip for two to the Brookfield Zoo in a Brinks armored car.

The money from Bond's wasn't that great, but it kept me fed and helped me repay many of my debts. It also gave me an opportunity to produce full-page flyers announcing the next dance, which we passed out at the end of each dance.

Prior to this, I got my art and typesetting done by outside artists. One artist was very reasonable, but he was too busy most of the time. The other artist was quite expensive, but he was generous enough to wait for his money, so I would occasionally use him.

But for the Teen Club I didn't need any great artwork, so I started doing it myself. I would use pieces of art supplied by an art service I subscribed to and typesetting that I would buy in sheet form and then press together letter by letter. I had watched my artists doing paste-ups before, so I got myself a T-square, some rubber cement, and a drawing board and became an artist. The Teen Club flyers gave me the experience, and I got better with every flyer I designed.

Around this time I was still doing work for Schuss Mountain, one of the ski resort advertising accounts. My other ski resort, Bryce's Mountain, refused to pay me $2,000 they owed me, claiming they never authorized certain ads. I had to file suit, which two years later I won by showing several letters of authorization they had issued me.

I also landed a new account. My former next-door neighbor in Oak Park called me up and asked me if I would mind working on a new car wash brochure his company was preparing.

I agreed and spent two solid months preparing the brochure for his company and having it printed for them. Although I had learned my lessons and had contracts with his company and made sure everything was in writing, as a stalling technique the company refused to pay the $10,000 they owed me. I sued them, only to have them go bankrupt on me. They were dishonest and I fell for their ploy.

I was still paying back the money I lost on the Teeny Bopper and the Batman credit card when this latest disaster hit. Now I was so broke, so much in debt, that I was seriously thinking of getting a job. Wendy and I got married at this time and she got a job while I prepared myself to look for one, too.

Things were probably at their lowest.

8
Pulling Ourselves Out

Wendy was now working and I was looking in the papers for a job at an advertising agency. It was the summer of 1968, around the time of the Chicago Democratic Convention.

A group I had hired at the Teen Club asked me if I wouldn't mind managing them and helping them cut a record. The idea appealed to me. I had observed dozens of bands and felt that the group that came to me was probably among the best. I had also had my experience with Mad Records and felt that maybe this time I would be luckier.

Cutting a hit record was one way to make it rich quick, and with my experience as a promoter and my need to make it rich or even make it to a point where I could pay off my debts, it was very tempting.

Through my contacts at the local radio station I got the name of Royal Disc Distributors, an honest record distributor and one that could give me good advice. So I prepared to go to downtown

Chicago for an interview with an ad agency and then, later, get some advice from the record distributor.

When I arrived at the Albert J. Rosenthal ad agency I was ushered into the office by one of the agency executives. He asked for a resume. I had none. I just had samples of my work. I had never had to get a job before so I never even thought of preparing a resume.

I showed him my work and he looked it over carefully. "What do you do?" he asked.

"I do copy, paste-up, typesetting—anything you need help in."

"But we're looking for someone who is very good at one skill. In an agency like ours, we would place you in one position and that would be the position you would grow in."

"Well, I could be a copywriter," I replied.

"Yes, but we're really looking for experience—agency experience, and I don't think you'll quite fit in."

So I left their offices. I was disappointed, but I quickly learned what I needed for an interview—a resume and some experience.

I have often thought to myself how my life and that of the Rosenthal agency would have changed if I had been hired. But I wasn't, and I left for my second appointment—at Royal Disc Distributing.

Royal Disc was owned by Kent Beauchamp and Edward Yalowitz—two young men in their thirties who were willing to give me advice on cutting records and promoting them. They weren't very encouraging, though. Apparently the record business wasn't that simple—something I had already discovered.

In the process of our discussions I explained what I did for a living and they asked me if I would mind spending the time reviewing their advertising and future promotion plans. I agreed.

Their office was located on Michigan Avenue, and I can remember driving that street during the days of the 1968 Democratic Convention with the National Guard on one side of the street and the protesters on the other side. But I didn't have time to stop or observe—I was too busy trying to survive.

I still had a quarter of a million Batman credit cards stored in the basement of my apartment building, along with assorted Teeny Boppers, Joe Subway records and car wash brochures. Life had definitely not been very kind to me. My job interview flopped, but I ended up with the opportunity to land another account.

The relationship with Royal Disc progressed well. Pretty soon they asked me to develop a corporate logo for a new company they had formed called Alltapes—a company organized to sell stereo tapes, which was a new, rapidly growing segment of the music industry.

Schuss Mountain was my other account. In my lawsuit against the car wash manufacturer I had met Joseph W. Smith, chief of the States' Attorney's Fraud and Complaint Division. Joe was impressed with my work and asked that I help him on his campaign as a representative for the Illinois Constitution Convention. Now, suddenly, with a few new accounts I was back in business. I soon started doing other political work for the Democratic Party while my involvement at Alltapes grew. Pretty soon I was doing a tremendous amount of work for Alltapes—so much so that they gave me my own office and asked me to troubleshoot a direct mail tape club they had started.

The orders were taking up to six weeks to fill and they didn't even know if they were making any money from the club. They had three people working on it with procedures that didn't make sense. It was a real mess.

Within three weeks I had worked out systems that permitted every order that came in the morning to get out that day. I had reduced the paperwork to the bare essentials, and I had reduced the staff to just two people.

Then I observed a very poor system they were using to pull tapes to fill their regular store orders. I called a special meeting of their entire organization and convinced them that they should change their entire warehouse and showed them how to do it. Within two weeks they had changed their system to mine.

Meanwhile, I produced a great deal of advertising for the

group, really putting their image in front of the financial community.

I involved myself in practically every aspect of their business. They used me as a consultant, as an advertising man, and I even organized many of their warehouse procedures. They put me on a retainer of $400 per week and they really got their money's worth.

They went public about this time and I bought $10,000 of their stock. By 1969 I had paid all my debts and had earned about $10,000 from my active work at Alltapes, so I felt that putting that money back into the company was a worthwhile investment. How could I lose? The stock market was making everybody wealthy. Now it was my turn.

Within a few months of my investment the stock dropped from $12 a share to $4 a share. It was my first experience with stocks and another failure I found hard to accept.

During my activities with Alltapes I did very well with all my other accounts, and if it hadn't been for the stock loss, I would have kept myself from getting into any trouble. I actually was earning about $30,000 a year—mostly tax-free as a result of my previous losses. And now Wendy and I were starting to save.

In 1970 Wendy and I decided to take a trip to England to visit Wendy's parents. We had also just bought a 1970 Oldsmobile station wagon—a big purchase for us at the time.

Things looked very good. We had some good accounts, I still had the Teen Clubs, and Wendy and I finally had a few dollars saved in the bank.

While we were in England Wendy and I spent about $3,000 on clothes and gifts—something we had denied ourselves during our years of struggling.

Upon our return we started looking for a home. Wendy was pregnant and we thought we'd find one before we had our first baby.

We did. But it was a lot more than we could afford. The house cost us $70,000 and at the time was a dream come true for us and a real steal. At that time houses weren't selling because we were in the midst of a recession. It had a huge basement, a garage, and, in fact, the whole house was awfully big for the little furniture we had in our small one-bedroom apartment.

With some financial help from my mom and a banking connection from my brother-in-law, I was able to squeak out a mortgage. But we were flat broke. Everything was gone—the money for the car, the trip to England plus the down payment— the mortgage took everything we had.

Then it really hit. The 1970 recession grew deeper and All-tapes needed to cut expenses.

I convinced them that they should cut out their stereo tape club. I showed them where they weren't making any decent profits and that the club wasn't worth the salary they were paying me. They responded not only by dropping the club, but by asking for my resignation. The recession was hitting them hard, and without the tape club, with few advertising requirements, and with the poor economy, it seemed a good move to them.

Since they represented over half my business, I had to carefully watch every penny. Not only did we have a new house to support, but we had a baby on the way.

Again, we were confronting financial problems, but thanks to a few of my accounts and my teen clubs, I was staying afloat.

9
Rock Group Promoter

In 1967 a rock group called the Dontays approached me to manage them. The group consisted of five guys who played the usual guitars, bass, and drums, but who could also play brass, piano, and flute. Each member had more than one function— whether it was playing two or three instruments or taking the lead singing assignment.

I was really impressed with the Dontays, and based on the groups I had seen, they seemed like one of the better groups in Chicago.

I agreed to handle them as their manager and I would get 10 percent of their earnings. They were getting $100 a performance and my first project was to get them a good booking agent and more money for their performances.

I took photos of them, created flyers and posters, and helped them get new equipment and a van to carry all their amplifiers and instruments.

The next thing I did was to get the names of all the other teen clubs that hired live groups. Then I created a newsletter called *The Chicagoland Teen Club Report*. Ten clubs got the report, along with a dozen booking agents and press people, but my motivation was not circulation.

I had a want ad section in my newsletter and put into it a series of free ads for other groups that needed bookings. The ads listed their fees—usually around $100. For the Dontays I listed a fee of $350.

About three issues of the newsletter had been published before I raised the price of the Dontays to $450. I would call each teen club owner to gather the news from the club, and they would see their names in print and cooperate the next time I called.

Finally, after about six issues, I raised the Dontay's salary to $650 and had my booking agent call the club owners to get them to book the group.

The booking agent would then cut a deal for a special "teen club owner's price" of $300. The deal was so good that nobody refused. From then on I was just building on their success, and by the end of the summer they were getting paid $1,000 a performance and were doing concerts with the Beach Boys and other famous groups. There was no secret that I was their manager, but I tried to get most of the deals through the booking agents so they would give the group some really good exposure. For the teen club owners, we kept the price at about $350.

About this time I took over a teen club in suburban Glen Ellyn. The club owner had been getting my newsletter and thought I could do a better job of promoting his club than he had been doing. As a result of the newsletter, I was also asked by a disc jockey to form a teen club with him in Aurora, Illinois, a small town about forty miles west of Chicago.

The disc jockey, Jim Stagg, had located an abandoned supermarket in a poor section of town and felt that with his connections the club would be a great success. He also felt his influence at getting top name groups at low prices would be very helpful.

So we met with the building owner, Zander Bowman, and agreed to test the facility for a few months. Stagg did very little other than show up for the dances and name the club the Graffiti, and I doubt if his influence helped book any groups or get them for anything less than I could have gotten them for.

For some reason the club wasn't successful. The room was so big that even an average crowd seemed small. If there is one thing the teens never liked, it was the feeling of a poor turnout, and no matter how successful a turnout we had, the room still looked empty. Since we named the place the Graffiti, we let the kids loose with marking pens and markers to decorate the walls, but that didn't help much.

The grand opening was a huge success. Over a thousand teens showed up for the three groups we booked. But then it was all downhill.

The neighborhood was bad and a number of neighborhood problems such as vandalism, rapes, and muggings didn't help things.

Meanwhile, we were losing money. The groups we were hiring were a lot more expensive than the club could support, and before we knew it, we were committed to groups a month in àdvance, with no hope of making any money on the program at all.

I had three teen clubs at the time: Frank Bond's in Berwyn, the Spectrum in Glen Ellyn, and the Graffiti in Aurora. I was taking all the money I was making at the Spectrum and Frank Bond's and covering my losses at the Graffiti.

Finally, Jim Stagg and I parted company and agreed to dissolve our partnership. The owner of the facility urged me to stay on and split the profits but not the risk. He would promote the club himself and all I had to do was book reasonably priced groups to keep our costs low. That didn't work either, and before a month went by I dropped the club completely and concentrated on the other two.

Shortly after I dropped the Graffiti, I was approached by Emerson Whitney, the new owner of the huge Aragon Ballroom on Chicago's north side. The Aragon used to be a plush Chicago landmark during the twenties, thirties, and forties, but the changing neighborhood, the deterioration of the facility, plus the general fading of interest in the big-time dance halls had all caused the Aragon to lose its popularity. It staged boxing matches instead of dances.

Whitney wanted me to do the promotion for the Aragon, which was going to start promoting rock shows. He had been one of my *Teen Club Report* subscribers and thought that I was the perfect guy to help promote his big shows.

He had a great sense of humor and was very shrewd when it came to knowing how to get publicity. One day, after spending two solid months getting all sorts of good publicity for the Aragon, I shot a picture of him lighting a cigarette for a performer in one of his acts. She wore a very, very low-cut dress, and I snapped the shot just as she was bending over Emerson's desk and he was lighting her cigarette.

The picture was really quite funny. It was a very suggestive picture of this girl and the smile and glint in Emerson's eyes made him look like he was really enjoying himself.

Knowing that Emerson had a great sense of humor, I had the shots developed and put a caption at the bottom of the photo as if I were preparing it for a publicity release. The caption read, "Light my fire. Emerson Whitney, Aragon owner, seems absolutely elated as he lights the cigarette of the lead singer of Johnny and the Greenmen now playing at the Aragon."

Emerson wasn't in when I brought it to his office, so I left it with his secretary with a note saying, "Here is that photo we released to all the newspapers today. They loved it and promised to use it."

I never sent it to the papers, nor would I without Emerson's approval. I knew he would realize this and would take the whole thing as a joke. But his wife happened to stop by the office after I left and saw this urgent-looking envelope lying on his desk. Mrs. Whitney was very conservative; she also did not have a very good sense of humor. She opened the envelope and the next day I was fired. Emerson had no choice.

The owner of the Spectrum in Glen Ellyn decided to close

down his club rather than renew his lease, so I was left with just Frank Bond's. I then tried an unsuccessful concert in Traverse City with the American Breed, which had played for me at Bond's and had already played quite successfully in Traverse City a few months before. I lost over $2,000 on that concert.

Finally, Frank Bond sold the banquet hall to another restaurant owner and the club was renamed Richard's, but soon attendance dropped because summer came; we agreed to close the club for the summer. I never reopened it and the facility was turned exclusively into a banquet hall.

That left me managing just the Dontays, and although they were doing well, it was obvious that they weren't going places unless we got them on records. About the time I had closed my clubs, I decided to get the Dontays a recording session and put them under contract, so I contacted a prominent Chicago attorney who specialized in working with artists.

The attorney, Dick Shelton, was very helpful in setting up all the contracts I needed, but he also put me in touch with Buck Ram, the producer of the Platters, the million-selling record group. Buck was trying to revive the Platters and was looking for a good Chicago publicist.

When I met Buck and his partner, Jean Bennet, we hit it off very nicely. They asked me to do some publicity for them and we agreed on a fee. I then told Buck about the Dontays and he agreed to hear them in concert and give me his opinion. He liked them and agreed to record them if we could raise the money for the session.

We raised the money, but the session never resulted in a hit. I pressed records and tried to have them played, but it was rough getting air time and the record never sold. On top of that, Buck never paid me for all the publicity I did for him and he disappeared once the record flopped.

The Dontays played a debutante coming-out party, and the daughter's father owned a radio station and a Cadillac dealership. He was so impressed with the group that he agreed to put up the funds for a record session and to use his station to promote the group. He was a tall Lincolnesque-looking man who had inherited his money mostly from his father; he appeared to be a shrewd businessman.

He had the Dontays spend two weeks recording his radio station jingles and then we signed a contract in which he was to take half ownership of the Dontays for $1,500. He agreed to record and promote them within a period of six months. After the jingle sessions, he wanted to back out of the deal and we refused. After all, the Dontays had done the equivalent of $3,000 worth of jingles and hadn't been paid a penny. So I sued him, and four years later I was awarded $1,500, which I gave to the Dontays. By the time I collected, it was 1974 and I was delighted to surprise the group with the bonus they had worked so hard for many years before.

10
Publicity

After my experiences in the record industry and with my teen clubs, I was in my new home and we had managed to make it through the winter without too much difficulty. Our first child was born in January, 1971. She was supposed to be born in February, so we named her April. You figure that one out.

My office was in one of the four bedrooms where I wrote my advertising and did my paste-ups. April kept me company in her crib while Wendy was typing my letters and retyping my copy.

I was really getting good at doing artwork and I was doing my own full-color brochures. Much of my work was now being done for various political candidates and for Schuss Mountain, which was still one of my major accounts.

I got along quite well with the resort's president, Daniel R. Iannotti, who put me in charge of the advertising and the publicity. I took a great deal of interest in the resort, often driving up there with Wendy during the ski season. I would write copy, conduct business, take pictures, and Wendy and I would do a little skiing.

After April was born our trips stopped and we had most of our contact with Dan over the phone. One day Dan called me and said, "Joe, our snowmobile program is not doing well. What can we do to encourage people to go snowmobiling here?"

I thought for a while and told him that I would call him back. This was 1971 and the women's lib movement was getting tremendous publicity.

It took me about an hour and I called Dan back. "Dan, let me read the release I just wrote. The headline is 'Resort Bans Women Snowmobilers,' and the story reads like this: Daniel R. Iannotti, president of the Schuss Mountain Ski Resort in Mancelona, Michigan, announced that he will no longer allow women to drive snowmobiles at his resort. Said Iannotti, 'If there's one thing worse than a woman driver, it's a woman snowmobiler.'"

Dan was a little taken aback. "But what about the protests we're going to get?" he said.

"So what? The worst that can happen is that you'll get more publicity," I replied.

Dan agreed. And I released the news item on the City News Bureau wires. The item immediately hit the national news wires and the news item was read on national TV news and radio and appeared in newspapers all over the country. Overnight Schuss Mountain's snowmobiling became the focus of national attention. Articles appeared in newspapers nationwide, and news commentators on network programs ended their news coverage with the item.

Now we braced ourselves for the onslaught of women protestors. But nothing happened. Only a few nasty notes. That's all. One week after the big publicity hit, I called Dan. "We can't let these women's lib groups do that to us."

"But Joe, they haven't done anything," Dan replied.

"That's just it," I said. "At least if they would have protested, we could have had more publicity. But that shouldn't stop us. You did get a few nasty notes, didn't you? Let's issue the following release:

WOMEN'S PROTESTS CAUSE BAN TO LIFT

Because of the pressure from Women's Lib groups upset over the recent ban against women snowmobilers, Daniel R. Iannotti, president of the Schuss Mountain Ski Resort in Mancelona, Michigan, has lifted his ban.' "

The second release made about half as much news as the first release did. But interestingly, it was the women reporters who were doing the interviewing and covering the story.

The publicity event gave the nation a lot of laughs, poked fun at the excesses of the women's lib movement, and drew so many snowmobilers to Schuss Mountain that their revenues were four times those of the previous month and stayed at that level for quite a few years.

Publicity has always been a fun game for me. I look at it as a creative challenge—a challenge to view and report the news in a different way or make the news fit the assignment.

During my years with Schuss, I was a member of the City News Bureau, which let me, for a fee, put my news releases on their news wire that would feed Chicago's media. Often the other wire services would pick up the stories, and TV and radio stations would soon follow.

Probably the biggest press conference I've ever conducted took place in a most unusual setting. I received a call one day from a young man, Earl Kitover, who had heard from my recording contract attorney that I was a good publicist. He wanted to talk to me about promoting his wife. Who was his wife? Miss Nude America, a popular exotic striptease dancer.

I invited him and his wife to our home to discuss their objectives. Apparently there was a big contest in Indiana at a nudist camp and the winner was Valorie Kitover. Earl Kitover had quit an engineering job to act as her manager.

Valerie was only getting a few hundred dollars a performance at the local clubs and Earl thought she deserved a lot more. He told me that with the right kind of publicity Valerie could command a thousand dollars a performance, but it took some major publicity to command that kind of fee.

Valerie definitely did not look like a stripper. She looked and acted like the neighbor next door—an innocent-looking, well-built, clean-cut girl whom you'd never expect to strip on stage at a striptease show.

But she did strip and Earl assured me that she'd do anything to get publicity—even dance in the nude if she had to.

Meanwhile, my wife was sitting there listening to the entire conversation in our den, thinking that the Kitovers had to rank as the weirdest account I'd ever had. I agreed to give their problem some thought and get back to them.

The next day I called Earl. "Earl, can Valerie perform at the Rialto?" I asked.

"Sure, they'd love to have her," he replied.

"Great. Get her a booking there and I'll do the rest. Are you sure she'll do anything?" I asked.

"Anything! You get her the publicity," he replied.

To get publicity for any politician in Chicago, all you had to do was attack Mayor Daley. But if you praised the mayor, not a word would appear in the papers. I realized this from handling many politicians during the past few years and knew what Chicago reporters would respond to.

I also knew that reporters would respond anyway to the story I was about to release to the City News Bureau. Imagine yourself a reporter for a Chicago paper seeing something like this come across the wires:

MISS NUDE AMERICA
CHALLENGES MAYOR DALEY

"Miss Nude America will conduct the city's first nude press conference in the basement of the Rialto Theatre in which she will announce her intentions to remove all her clothes on stage at the Rialto Theatre to challenge Mayor Daley's nudity ordinance."

I have conducted several news conferences in my life for everything from politicians to products, but never have I had such a large turn-out as I did for this one. Everybody was there.

I even had reporters from the *Wall Street Journal* with cameras, even though the *Journal* has never printed a photograph in their history. The TV news people were there from every Chicago TV station—including an educational channel and two I never knew existed.

But Mayor Daley was not to be undone by Miss Nude America. Although he had succeeded in successfully challenging more formidable opponents, Miss Nude America presented a totally different threat. He responded by sending the fire department to inspect the Rialto for fire violations, and the fire inspectors found several.

However, when the fire inspectors saw the big press turnout, they realized that to disappoint the press would cause more headlines. After a few calls to key city officials, the situation was reassessed and the Rialto got just a warning.

Meanwhile, the press gathered outside Valerie's dressing room (or, should we say, undressing room) and had their cameras ready and their notebooks out.

Finally, Valerie emerged, just as promised, wearing only her high-heeled shoes. Her figure left no doubt about how she had won the Miss Nude America contest. I can remember a pause when she stepped up to the microphone as the reporters prepared for probably their most unusual press conference. The only sounds you could hear were the whirring of seven TV cameras and the strobe lights flashing.

Valerie stepped up to the microphone to read a prepared statement I had written for her the day before. She read it as if she were a high school student standing before her class reciting a composition. She seemed as innocent and as naive as the little girl next door, and I'm sure that also took the reporters by surprise. Her statement was really a rehash of our press release, so there was nothing new, but it was important that a formal announcement break the ice. From then on, it was downhill all the way.

She then announced she would take questions from the reporters. With every question I started to look for a hole to crawl in. For example, when asked why she was doing it, she answered honestly, "I want to get enough publicity so I can charge more for my exotic dancing." After this disarming answer, the questions continued.

There was no doubt that the reporters were enjoying the answers and, quite frankly, they probably couldn't have cared less. Cameras were shooting photos that would never see the pages of any newspaper. TV news cameras were taking footage that viewers would not be permitted by law to view.

After her press conference she went back into the dressing room, put her clothes on, and proceeded on stage to undress before the thinnest crowd ever to attend the Rialto. Apparently nobody wanted to be in the audience with all that publicity except the handful of reporters—all in the line of duty.

The next day Valerie was front page news in all four Chicago newspapers and on all the TV shows. All the papers and TV newscasts showed was her portrait and not much more.

Later her price went up to $1,500 a performance and she was Chicago's top stripper, an honor directly related to her Chicago publicity campaign. The Rialto closed down shortly after that. Valerie now has a baby and Earl, her husband, has a job as an accomplished inventor.

I handled other publicity during this time, as it proved to be the least expensive way to advertise my clients' products or services. I did publicity for the Spot Restaurant in Evanston, north of Chicago. I was doing their advertising and the restaurant owner, Jerry Herman, told me that his dream was to get some publicity on the Johnny Carson show.

One day on the air Johnny Carson started kidding Ed McMahon, who claimed that mayonnaise originated as a result of his distant relatives.

I saw an opportunity to capitalize on the statements. I immediately prepared a label for a large jar of mayonnaise and called it Ed McMahon Mayonnaise. In the ingredients we listed 5 percent alcohol to add to the ribbing that Carson always gave

McMahon. I also listed a whole series of humorous instructions that tied into the show and sent Carson a letter from the Spot about the product's popularity. I did mention a problem, however. The stuff couldn't be served in Evanston because alcohol was not allowed in the North Shore community. Evanston was dry.

Carson gave three minutes to the bit and the Spot was deluged with calls and customers for a week.

Another time, Herman wanted me to come up with a different promotion. His specialty was pizza. A new fad was taking hold at this time: Women were not only going all out for women's lib, but they were removing their bras as a sign of their independence. So I suggested the world's first bra-shaped pizza, which consisted of two round pizzas connected by a few straps. It, too, made the Chicago papers.

Around this time Spiro Agnew was becoming a household name. In fact, Agnew's name was unknown before the 1968 political conventions and Nixon's statement "Agnew is no household name" was often bantered around.

So I created a series of products, some of which included Spiro Agnew facial tissue, toilet paper, drain cleaner—an entire line of Spiro Agnew household products. Then I sent out the release. I really had no client to promote and quite frankly didn't intend to promote the product anyway. But I thought it would give the public a good laugh and be perfect for those humorous bits at the end of the news shows. Hopefully, the publicity would land me a new client.

Sure enough, it got good national coverage, but I quickly discovered something about making fun of politicians. I got bomb threats, people calling me up and yelling at me. It wasn't much fun after all, and I didn't get any new clients.

I've also had some promotions destroyed because of poor timing. The Teeny Bopper promotion was a good example, but I've had others that were just as bad.

I've released a promotion the same day that four major news stories broke, each one of which would have rated a huge front page headline by itself. The paper that day had four large headlines and my big story was totally ignored.

Then I had a front page picture in the Chicago *Sun-Times* yanked the hour Eisenhower died in 1969. The picture did run, but only in the earliest editions of the paper.

Publicity was always lots of fun and I never lost my shirt, as I did with my other paid promotions.

11
Politics,
the Tooth Fairy,
and the Calculator

After losing Alltapes, my biggest account, I started to look for additional clients. I moved my small operation to a second story bedroom in my home and set up a small office.

It was 1971 and the recession was in full swing when I got a call from Dick Orkin, the talent who had created Chickenman and who originally had produced my Batman radio spots.

Dick had created another radio series, called "The Tooth Fairy," for his own newly formed company. He wondered if I'd be interested in creating all the promotional material for the series. Each radio station that bought the program would want to promote the show and give away bumper stickers, buttons— the same stuff we used for our Great Teeny Bopper Society.

The deal was simple. I would own part of a company called The Tooth Fairy Company and we would split the costs of producing the materials and split the profits.

I accepted and started to design and produce the materials. I then sent mailings to all the radio stations carrying the program. I sent samples of the T-shirts, the bumper stickers, and the buttons.

In a very short time we realized that the world was not going crazy for the "I Believe in the Tooth Fairy" goodies we were trying to peddle, and we abandoned the project. Although the show was popular, the promotional items never did go over too well. Dick and I parted on the best of terms.

There wasn't any money lost on the project—just a lot of valuable time. But I had enough work with my political candidates, the Schuss Mountain Ski Resort, and a few restaurant accounts to pay my mortgage and generate enough money to buy a photo typositor—a new typesetting machine for my small advertising agency.

It was now spring of 1971 and I was heavily involved with the gubernatorial campaign of Thomas A. Foran, the former chief government prosecutor of the Chicago Seven trial in Chicago. His assistant in the trial was Richard Schultz—my brother-in-law. Dick recommended me to Tom Foran and I became the campaign's advertising man.

In the process of the campaign I noticed that a few of his assistants were using an electronic calculator they had rented to total up the campaign statistics.

I asked to borrow the large Sharp brand desk-top unit, which I took home to try. I used it to figure out my mark-ups, add up my charges, and compute discounts, and I found it to be a tremendous time-saving tool for my agency. I was going to buy one until I discovered that the unit sold for $600—a little more than I could afford at the time.

The Foran campaign continued. I was producing beautiful campaign literature and doing excellent photography, but Foran's efforts weren't paying off and I was replaced by a few other advertising people who didn't save him either. Foran's campaign was designed to convince Mayor Daley to select him to run for governor, yet Foran couldn't muster enough support to get Daley's backing and eventually dropped out.

My political advertising activity was quite successful, even with the Foran loss. They said that if more than 60 percent of your candidates won, you were a good advertising man. My record was 87.5 percent winners—an incredible record. But there was a catch. Fifty percent of my winners were eventually either indicted or sent to prison—but then that was Chicago politics.

One day while glancing through *Business Week* magazine, I came across an article about a pocket calculator that would sell for $240 and would add, subtract, multiply, and divide.

I thought about my desire to own one of those units and called the manufacturer. After about $26 in phone calls, I finally reached Craig Corporation in Compton, California. I expressed my interest in their new pocket calculator and asked if our agency could introduce the product through a direct mail campaign. I talked to a Lauren Davies who was their national sales manager.

I told Lauren that I could tell him very quickly, through my testing, whether or not the pocket calculator would sell. The idea intrigued Craig's marketing people. They weren't sure whether the product would sell and we gave them a good test vehicle. They had a representative who happened to have one of the first prototype samples with him, and he would be instructed to stop by and pay me a visit.

Alex Molnar, a solf-spoken, slim man in his forties, stopped by my home. It was October of 1971, and Alex presented me with my first pocket calculator. I looked it over and asked him if I could buy it, giving Alex a check for $141.

I told Alex that first I wanted to show it to a client of mine for a possible direct mail advertising campaign, and that I would get back to him within a few days.

I brought the calculator to my former client at Alltapes. I showed them the unit, demonstrated it, and asked Kent Beauchamp if he thought a mailing to his stereo tape club list was a good idea.

"Who would pay $240 for a pocket calculator that nobody

heard of through the mail yet?" said Kent. "I don't wanna take a chance."

So I drove home thinking what a great opportunity it would be for me to try. But I was still struggling to make a living, and with a baby I had other responsibilities to consider. I couldn't take a chance.

All my life I've always had people telling me, "Joe, if you ever need investors, let me know. One of these days you'll strike it rich." But I never had the guts to ask anybody for money, and thank goodness—I would have made many people poorer.

When I arrived home I received a call from Ed Bauman. Ed was a forty-year-old real estate salesman who also managed a rock group called the Family. Ed's group played at my clubs and I used to sympathize with his problems of managing rock groups who never appreciated their managers.

He was trying to interest me in a possible real estate deal. I told him that I couldn't afford the money, but I asked him if he'd like to double his money within a few short months.

"Great," he said. "What's the deal?"

I described the pocket calculator and the economics of direct mail. "Ed, most direct mailings have a 2-percent response rate. With the pocket calculator deal, a 2-percent response will double our money the first week. How would you like to be an investor?"

Ed got all excited and drove out to my home, where I showed him the unit. "With just a simple mailing piece, and renting just the right lists, we could easily double our money," I assured him.

The deal I worked out was simple. I told Ed that I needed $12,000 for the campaign. If he would raise the money, I would agree that the first profits to come in would go to him and his investors until he doubled his money and his investors got a 50-percent return on their money. Then I would make the rest. I would also own the business and have no further responsibility to the group after our goals were met.

Ed agreed and I presented my concept to a group of his friends. We raised $12,000 and I proceeded to rent 50,000 names using ten different mailing lists. I rented a list of 5,000 accountants, 5,000 engineers—all the people who I thought could use a calculator.

I raced to print the full-color flyer and letter and got Craig Corporation to start shipping me calculators in November.

I had all my forms ready to go. I bought a tape machine to seal the packages and Wendy bought plenty of stamps. Wendy and I were going to work together to open the mail, and although I felt that we could handle everything ourselves, I knew that there would come a day when we'd have to get help if my little mail order company succeeded.

I had named my new company the JS&A National Sales Group. I already called my advertising agency "JS&A Advertising," an abbreviation for Joseph Sugarman and Associates, so I was able to use the same letterheads and answer the phone the same way.

The mailing went out and I waited for the response. All I needed was a two-tenths-of-one-percent return to break even. Later we discovered that our company was the first to introduce this untested, unproven product—a product that launched the micro-electronic revolution.

I'll never forget the first response I received. My feeling at the time was, "Ya mean somebody would buy a $240 calculator through the mail?" It just seemed so incredible that the concept worked—but did it? I needed a lot greater response than one order.

But the final response was poor. After a dozen or so orders, I realized, based on projections, that we were going to lose half of our money.

Here, the first time I had attempted to get investors for a venture it ended in failure. I would have to confront them with the sad results.

To prepare for the meeting I decided to run an analysis of the response. In testing the ten lists I gave each reply card a special code that corresponded to the mailing list I used. To my surprise, I discovered that two of the lists were actually successful and that the others were so bad that they brought down the total overall response. The two lists were the last two I had selected.

I remember Jim Pheta, my list salesman, telling me to try the presidents of million-dollar corporations, which I thought was a rather stupid choice. Certainly engineers and accountants would respond in droves, but presidents of big corporations didn't have time to read advertising literature sent through the mail from unknown companies.

But I accepted Jim's suggestion, and to my amazement, he was right. The only successful lists were the last two I selected and the two I would have never expected to succeed.

After my analysis I saw that had I used just those two lists, I could have doubled my investors' money and made a profit myself. The calculator was selling for $240 and costing me around $140, so I made a little less than $100 per unit after the credit card charges were deducted. We were using Master Charge, Bank Americard, and American Express, although most of the orders came in with a check.

"If only I could convince my investors to stay in," I thought, "I know we could make it."

But Ed Bauman needed some of his money back and his investors were pestering him, trying to find out the results. I had to move quickly.

On a hunch I called Craig Corporation and talked again to Lauren Davies, the national sales manager. He was anxious to find out the results of our campaign, so I leveled with him. "Lauren, it didn't go too well, but we did discover the types of people who would buy the calculator." I then proceeded to describe my findings.

Lauren advised me that I could sell the calculator for $180 because the costs were starting to drop. The new price of $103 would be effective February 1.

When I got my group of investors together, I told them of my results, of the new price, and of the excellent chance we had of succeeding. "If you guys decide to back out, I'll definitely continue on my own," I said.

They all agreed to stay in after a brief series of questions. It was now December and most of the responses were in. Indeed we had lost half the money. Even if my investors wanted back what was left of their money, I probably would have eventually paid all their money back anyway.

The mailing I wanted to conduct included a million names. The 10,000 names that worked were taken from a list of a million names that I had great confidence would work. The $6,000 that was left would just cover about 25,000 mailing pieces, and yet if I was going to score big, I had to roll my campaign out quickly and in great numbers to beat the competition.

I was thirty-three years old, just barely able to pay my mortgage, and had a wife and child to support. I knew that each time in my life that I had felt I had a sure winner, something came up at the last minute and grasped success from me just as I felt it was within reach. I knew that if I invested the huge sums of money I needed to make this program a success and lost, it might be a blow I wouldn't recover from for years.

I realized that I'd risk my home, my car, and everything I owned if my mailing failed. And with my luck, something was sure to happen that I least suspected but would certainly end up in disaster.

I remember the confusion that I felt at the time. Having nobody to turn to for advice, I called Harvey Wagley, president of United Letter Service. I had first met Harvey at the Schuss Mountain annual stockholders' meeting. He was a Schuss stockholder and ran a large mailing house called United Letter Service.

I had used United Letter Service for my first mailing, so I called Harvey for advice. Harvey was in his sixties, a tall thin man who talked loudly and who had started his large business in a small downtown office over forty years earlier. He was a genuine entrepreneur, self-taught and with a wisdom that comes only from years of experience and years of learning.

I explained my problem to Harvey and he made a few suggestions: "Why not a 400,000 mailing instead of a million, and if it doesn't succeed, well, you'll take a lot longer to pay me back. Just don't worry about it."

Since Harvey was also willing to pay for the postage, the major bulk of my expenses would rest with his company. I think he also knew that I'd eventually pay him back, and he seemed to take a great deal of pride in helping other entrepreneurs get into business.

I accepted his offer and proceeded to order the mailing lists, envelopes, and printing. I remember the big lump I felt in my stomach as I ordered all of this material. I was already conditioned to fear the worst, but a hundred thousand dollars was a lot of money to be playing with.

United Letter Service dropped the mailing at the post office in early January, 1972, and I waited for the response. Ten days went by and Wendy and I made sure that everything was in supply. We had calculators, stamps, a filing system, forms, and everything we could possibly need for what we hoped would be the big response.

I also had a contractor give me an estimate on what it would cost to convert my basement into a work area should I need more room than my garage and my upstairs bedroom.

Finally, the response started to trickle in, then pour in, then it literally started to gush in. There were more responses than Wendy and I could possibly handle—more, in fact, than I could possibly imagine.

I called up a temporary service for help and was sent three women to assist me. I called the contractor and told him to finish the basement as soon as he could because it looked as if I'd be needing it soon. And finally, I called Harvey Wagley to assure him that he'd get his money back and called my investors and told them the good news, too.

I now had a business. I finally succeeded in probably my biggest gamble to date, and once again I could feel comfortable that my mortgage would be paid and I wouldn't have to live in poverty—at least for a little while.

I was now using practically every room in the house to process orders. The only place I didn't use was our own bedroom, but with the other three bedrooms being used, along with the living room, kitchen and garage, Wendy was getting a little concerned.

Our home was no longer our home. It was a factory processing orders and shipping calculators. One of the temporaries, a woman named Mary Ann Haire, started during this time and still works part time for us today. Many of our original suppliers also still trade with us. It was the start of JS&A, and the first phase of a new and rapidly emerging mail order company.

Projecting our gains, it looked as if I'd be left with $50,000 from the results of our campaign. I found out that we were selling more calculators than Sears, which was also carrying the product, but because of its needs, Craig Corporation was not filling our orders fast enough. We were the first to introduce the pocket calculator in November, and we had convinced Craig that the calculator would be a real winner in January, 1972.

12
Our First Mail Order Ad

The very first space ad we placed appeared in the *Wall Street Journal*. And like many of my experiences, it wasn't easy.

I was rather surprised by the sudden drop in calculator prices from $240 to $180 and had heard rumors that a drop to $100 was possible in the very near future. Rumors spread that the new $100 price point wasn't too far off.

The problem in marketing a calculator through direct mail was the time it took to conduct a campaign. Sure, I had the mailing piece that worked and a good idea of which mailing lists would work, but to produce large quantities of envelopes and mailing pieces, have them stuffed and then wait for the post office to deliver them might take months. The fear of having my mailing piece ready for the mails and having the prices drop stopped me from continuing in what was starting to become a successful formula.

The next logical step was an advertisement in the *Wall Street*

Journal. Here was a national newspaper that printed an advertisement a few days after receipt. It was the fastest, most
efficient way to hit the largest number of middle- to upper-
income executives—the same type of consumer that responded to
my mailing.

The next problem was to translate that entire mailing piece—
including the letter, circular, order card, and full-color image—
into an advertisement in black and white—one that would hold
the readers' interest, explain the product, and close the sale.

I took all the elements of that mailing piece, used a different
approach, and ended up with a piece of copy that included all
the things a good direct mail piece should have. I reduced the
size of the pictures and concentrated on the copy. My theory was
that if a reader was interested enough in a product, he would
read the entire ad. And if I could convince him with simple,
basic, honest language that what we offered was indeed the best
product and value, then I could ask for the order.

My theory was based on my experiences in the fifties. I
remember when the new cars would roll out. At that time it was
really an exciting event. Car styles changed rapidly and the car
companies made such hoopla that fall turned into an exciting
period for car enthusiasts.

I also remember picking up those new car brochures that
showed full-color shots of the cars but little descriptive copy. The
copy was written to create a mood, a feeling about the car, but
nothing more. I had often thought that Detroit had missed the
boat. If I were to write a car brochure today instead of saying
that a car had "rack and pinion steering," I would explain what
rack and pinion steering was, how it worked, and why my
system was better than anyone else's. Detroit missed providing a
real consumer service back in the fifties.

Will people read all that copy? If it's kept simple enough,
informative, and if there is a genuine interest in the product,
people will read and read and read and read.

After two days of rewriting, I sat down at my photo typositor
and set the headlines, while my wife diligently set the type on

our IBM Selectric Composer. I then proceeded to make my paste-up for what turned out to be a four-column-by-sixteen-inch ad.

When I finished the advertisement, I called the *Wall Street Journal* and spoke to Lauren Commotore, the salesman in charge of small accounts. I found out that in order to run an advertisement, I had to fill out credit forms and provide references.

While that was pending, I reserved the back page of the *Journal*. I knew that sometimes, when I didn't have time to read the entire issue, I would scan the front and back pages. So, I figured I'd have better response if I ran my ad on the back page.

We filled out the forms and waited for final approval from the *Journal*. The target date was approaching, but still no confirmation. Lauren then called me about three days before the ad was to break with the news that they'd need a check in advance. Apparently my credit lines weren't sufficient to allow a $10,000 charge. Lauren had to rush out to my home, pick up the check, and release the go-ahead to run the ad.

Meanwhile I was preparing for the response. I had the telephone company install three new lines, the lock company put deadbolt locks on all our doors, and I hired an armed guard to stand by just in case.

My garage was loaded with about 250 calculators, the cars were cleared out, and our garage shipping department was ready to go.

All the while, our basement was under construction and the phone company was prewiring it for up to twelve lines. We were already using practically every room in the house to process orders, type labels, and ship, so the place was really busy.

I also felt that it was time to hire a permanent secretary to relieve my wife of some of her responsibilities. We placed an ad in the paper and, after talking to a dozen women, selected one named Mary Stanke to work for us. Mary was looking for a part-time job—something from 9 A.M. to 3 P.M.—so she could spend time with her two children who returned home from school around 3 P.M. I offered her $3.25 an hour to start and she seemed pleased and was going to start on February 28, 1972—the day our first *Wall Street Journal* ad was to break. Mary has worked with me ever since.

Meanwhile Alex Molnar, the Craig representative, wanted to see the action when the ad broke, so I put him on a chair by a phone to answer the phone calls.

Two days before the ad broke in the *Journal*, a discount house in the East advertised in a small ad, "Coming Soon—Craig 4501 Calculator, Only $139.00."

From the last minute pressures of getting everything ready, to getting the confirmation from the *Journal*, and seeing the discount ad, I'd say that this had to be one of the most tense times of my life. To top it off, my one-year-old daughter, April, fell down the basement steps the evening before the ad broke. As we brought her bloodied body to the hospital, I knew I was really being put through a test. April was okay and fortunately nothing serious happened, but I certainly felt that I was paying my dues.

13
Providing a Service

That first advertisement in the *Wall Street Journal* was a real thrill for me. A few days after it ran, we began to get orders. The phones were busy, my staff was working hard, and Mary Stanke was darting from room to room coordinating the activity.

In just ten days I had made $20,000. Not only was the response fast, but heavy as well. I had never in my life made so much money so quickly. It was too good to be true.

I was about to run more ads when I got a call from Peter Behrendt, president of Craig Corporation. He told me that my advertisement caused his regular dealers to call his company and demand that they get adequate inventories of the calculator.

I was getting 50 percent of Craig's production—more than any other dealer including Sears—and as a result of my ad, Craig Corporation would have to cut off our shipments and allocate a very small percentage to us.

I was really upset. Here was my big opportunity to take

79

advantage of everything I had done to build for this moment—including creating the original demand for the unit—and now it was being taken away from me.

I had never been in a back-order position with the calculator and orders were still coming in, with very little inventory to back it up.

It wasn't until April of that year that we finally filled all our back orders, but by then it was too late. Calculator prices had dropped to $129.95 and the chances of our company succeeding at $179.95 were slim.

We did try once again in a regional edition of the *Wall Street Journal* in April and got one order from the ad. It was time to go to my next product.

During 1972 and 1973, I concentrated on the new wave of calculators and digital watches. I concentrated all our advertising in just the *Wall Street Journal* and I concentrated on the very same format, advertisement after advertisement.

A few ads were extremely successful, others were average, and some were unsuccessful. I found, however, that all I needed were a few successes to offset my many failures—so, like the gambler who continues to roll the dice, I kept rolling, but the dice always paid off at the end. The ads that seemed the most successful were those in which I told everything about a product—even the disadvantages. Soon I discovered that honesty in advertising was the most effective tool I could use in selling a product. In fact, it was the same lesson I had learned from my teen clubs.

In April of 1972, just as we were catching up with our back orders on our first pocket calculator, we moved into the basement. The carpenters, the rug installers, the painters were all through. Our staff was down to just Mary Ann Haire, our first temporary employee, and Mary Stanke, our first full-time employee. The big explosion was over. Our business had wound down considerably.

Operating out of the basement was really one of the most enjoyable phases of my business career. Mary Stanke would arrive at 8:30 in the morning, ring the bell, and go down the stairs to the basement. Mary Ann Haire would follow. And I'd roll out of bed a few minutes before 8:30 and grope my way down the stairs to my desk.

The basement was where we processed all our orders, accepted the returned packages, and handled the customer service functions. We commissioned a company to warehouse our products and ship from the labels we supplied. Things were really quite simple and quiet except for those occasional telephone calls from customers in a rush to get a product or two.

By February of 1973 calculator prices had plummeted to $69.95 and the public was really confused. I knew they were because I would often get calls from people asking all sorts of questions, worried if we were in store for another price drop and wondering which calculator to buy.

So I took out a large ad that ran on the back page of the *Wall Street Journal* entitled "The Truth About Pocket Calculators." There were no pictures, no subheadlines—just 3,000 words of very interesting copy. The purpose of the ad was to inform and educate the consumer on how to buy a pocket calculator.

I talked about features, the floating decimal, the constant key. I discussed prices, where the units were manufactured, and even predicted the future. Then I honestly told consumers where they could buy calculators and gave them three options: department stores, discount stores, and mail order companies, giving the advantages and disadvantages of each. I ended the ad with the words, "See our other ad in this issue of the *Journal*." The other ad showed five calculators that we were offering—all priced very competitively.

After the ad broke we were literally deluged with mail praising us for the public service we had provided and including orders for calculators that, within a few weeks, reached a sales volume of $250,000. We got a tremendous number of letters that asked us questions—after all, the advertisement clearly gave consumers the impression that we knew our business and they came to us in droves with their questions.

There was so much mail that it was delivered in sacks and we spent many hours late in the evening sorting it and answering the huge response.

It was during that promotion that I realized the reason for the success of most businesses: simply that a business provides a service, and the more service it provides, the more responsive the market. Consumers appreciated the service I provided and they responded—all successful businesses owe their success to this very simple principle.

During 1972 and 1973, we'd often get consumers who would call up and give us their credit card numbers on the phone to expedite their shipments. At first we held our breath, hoping that nobody would deny that they had ordered something and leave us holding the bag.

But after a full year of operating this way without any problems, we decided to try an experiment. We included a toll-free 800 number in our ad and told consumers that they could order on the phone using their credit cards. The response was incredible. By noon the first day we had already broken even on our ad and the orders were piling in. The toll-free credit card concept not only provided an additional service to consumers, making it easier for them to shop, but it also sold more product.

For one year we used the toll-free number in our advertisements without any competition. Everybody watched us, but nobody wanted to try this new form of marketing. Finally they caught on, and by the fall of 1974 just about every mail order company was using toll-free numbers to take credit card orders.

In the years to come, an entire industry evolved from the concept. Answering services that did nothing but take toll-free orders sprang up everywhere. WATS line usage mushroomed, and catalogs and TV offers everywhere were predominately displaying toll-free 800 numbers.

14
The Watergate Scandal

The Watergate scandal made quite an impact on our nation. It also made quite an impact on Joe Sugarman. As an involved American, I had three experiences worth relating about this very historic period.

The first took place in 1972—well before the election that November. A lawyer I met through one of my political advertising accounts had a serious problem and asked if I knew anyone who could help him.

Very simply, he needed someone to bug his law partner's office because he suspected that his partner was cheating him. The lawyer did not know that I had actually done that type of work while I was in the army. I told him of my experience and I explained to him that although I could probably do the job, it was illegal and I would rather put him in touch with someone else. I had just started my successful new business in my basement; I was quite busy, and besides, I didn't want to violate the law.

The lawyer, whose name I won't mention for obvious reasons agreed to have me find somebody for him and I looked in the telephone directory for a store that sold an unusual German tape recorder called a UHER. This was the same type of recorder the intelligence community used to record signals from their eavesdropping devices. The stores that sold these devices were good places to find the name of a detective or a "manufacturer" of bugs. Incidentally, the UHER was the same tape recorder that caused that 18½-minute gap in President Nixon's Watergate tapes.

After a personal visit to the tape recorder store, I was able to obtain the name of a character who actually made the bugs. I went over to his sleazy operation on the first floor of an apartment building on Chicago's north side and talked to him.

At first he was cold and brief with me, but using intelligence-type talk, I soon convinced him that I was for real and he finally opened up—bragging about what a great job he did and telling me that half the bugs produced and planted in Chicago were his. He was so open and such a braggart that quite frankly I didn't believe him.

Anyone operating in such a shady illegal business would certainly keep his activities quiet, but not this character. I became concerned about having him plant the bug for my lawyer friend for fear he'd brag to some undercover police officer.

The character, whom we'll call J.D., agreed to meet with my friend and plant the bug. I arranged the meeting, warning my friend that I was not impressed with J.D. but felt that we couldn't be too choosy and he was free to work out his own deal and free to assume his own risks. My friend thanked me.

That day I had read about the Watergate break-in at the Democratic headquarters in Washington. When I called J.D. to give him the meeting address, he started bragging to me that it was his bug they found at the Watergate Hotel.

"Sure, J.D., you really do get around," was my sarcastic reply.

My second Watergate experience started when it was revealed

that Nixon recorded his telephone conversations. The newspapers played the story up so much that it even gave credibility to the act of tape recording phone conversations. The reasoning went, if Nixon could do it, so could any American.

So I quickly rounded up three tape recorders and three telephone pick-up devices. The phone pick-up devices were nothing elaborate—you just attached them to the tape recorder and put a ring-shaped device around the earpiece of the phone. This would let you record phone conversations legally since it was clearly explained that Nixon did not violate the law. As long as one of the two parties knew the conversations were being recorded, it was legal.

I wrote an ad entitled, "Tap Your Phone" clearly explaining that President Nixon had made recording of phone conversations an accepted practice. I urged businessmen to consider the recording of phone conversations as another form of business record-keeping and then offered three recording systems in the ad.

The ad ran and it wasn't successful. We sold only a few units and did not even break even. Worse, however, was the reaction at the *Wall Street Journal*. They refused to run the ad again and threatened to drop us as an advertiser if we ever ran anything like it again. If that wasn't bad enough, I got a call from the FBI. They wanted to talk to me.

When the agent arrived, I escorted him into my basement, we sat down, and we chatted. He explained that his primary interest was in determining if my equipment could be used for surreptitious recording, which is illegal. I assured him it wasn't and explained the premise for my advertisement.

The agent was quite reasonable and could see from my basement operation and the other advertisements that we were a reputable company and that our products were not violating the law—simply capitalizing on some Watergate publicity.

As we talked, the topic turned to Watergate and I asked the investigator if they knew who had made the Watergate bug. If you'll recall the story, it was the bug that actually started the

Watergate scandal. The bug went bad and prompted the con-
spirators to replace or repair it. It was then that they were
caught.

The agent said, "We know exactly who planted the bug."

I asked, "If I tell you his initials will you tell me if it was the
same guy?"

The agent agreed and I said, "Was it J.D.?"

The agent nodded his head. "Yep, he is the guy," and then
mentioned his actual name.

"Why wasn't he arrested?" I asked. The agent explained that
the FBI had more important things to do, although I suspect
that J.D. probably bragged to them in return for immunity.
Maybe the FBI didn't care but, regardless, the same guy was
working for my friend.

Later I checked with my friend and discovered that indeed he,
too, had problems with his bug, but eventually it did work and
he got his information. Thank goodness he wasn't caught.

I mentioned earlier that I had three experiences with the
Watergate scandal. Unfortunately, the last one cost me a lot
more than the first two.

It was May of 1973 when I traveled to Los Angeles to meet
with a supplier. He had invited me to stay at his home and
watch the Chicago Blackhawks play in the Stanley Cup finals,
which were blocked out on Chicago television.

My supplier's name was Howard and the first time we had
done business was in 1972 when I introduced his product in a
major advertising campaign. I eventually found out that Howard
was not totally honest with me and that he had shipped me
defective merchandise that caused a heavy return rate and
eventually a large loss for my new company. JS&A has since
developed a very strong quality control system.

Howard was inviting me to Los Angeles to explore the possibility of buying all his remaining inventory and to let me see a
few new ideas he had. I also planned to see a few more of my
suppliers during the trip.

Howard was an enthusiastic, intense, fast-talking ex-New

Yorker who seemed to have unlimited energy. I always marveled at his enthusiasm and drive, which caused me to overlook his worst character trait—his dishonesty.

Howard and I had dinner, which his wife served, and then Howard and I retired to the living room of his two-bedroom apartment.

We were relaxing, watching the NBC national evening news to hear the latest Watergate developments, which were sounding more and more like daytime soap opera. Every night, a new discovery, revelation, or indictment was announced, and the continuing story was now dominating the news.

That evening, however, seemed to be the most depressing. It was announced that John Mitchell and John Ehrlichman had been indicted in the Watergate scandal—an indictment that truly shocked the nation. "What next?" I asked, as Howard just sat there in silence.

"I don't know," was his reply. "It just doesn't make sense anymore."

"Ya know, Howard, the timing's perfect for a Watergate game," I said. "The rules could be a riot."

Howard jumped up. "Wow, what a great idea! Sure, a Watergate game! Brilliant idea! Let's do it."

And so the Watergate scandal game was born that May evening in Howard's apartment in Redondo Beach, California—a suburb of Los Angeles.

Howard and I stayed up until late in the evening developing our plans. I developed the game, the rules, and the instructions, while Howard drew up the marketing and public relations plans. We were to be partners and my job was to get the cards produced while Howard lined up the sales.

The game was quite clever. The box proclaimed, "A game of cover-up and deception for the whole family," and consisted of cards with such names as Phone Tapper, Campaign Chief, Hired Saboteur, Presidential Advisor, and Attorney General. The wild card was the Attorney General's wife.

The object of the game was to cover up and cheat, but if you got caught, you picked a penalty card that assigned you a number of points. The more points you received, the bigger loser you were. Penalties included one hundred points for being indicted, fifty points for being exposed by the press, and no points for being a big contributor—just as in real life.

Some of the lines used in the instructions included: "This game may be further enhanced by playing it in such places as under a table, behind closed doors, and on dark street corners. Although the game is not intended for gambling purposes, passing the buck is perfectly O.K. Players have been known to bribe the dealer, stack the deck, remove and destroy important cards, and 'bug' other players."

My first job was to get somebody to print a few thousand decks right away. When I arrived home I worked through the night to do all the artwork and typesetting for the card game, the box, and the instructions. Meanwhile Howard started contacting the public relations firm, lining up the publicity appearances and a national TV tour for both of us.

I located a card manufacturer, convinced him that we needed the cards immediately, and he cooperated. Within ten days we had performed a miracle. Not only did we have the cards, but we had the box as well. Meanwhile the PR firm arranged a big press conference for us at the Watergate in Washington where we were going to unveil the game for the first time.

Before the press conference, Howard called me up all excited. "Joe, they're going crazy over this idea. Everybody wants to buy the game. The stores are clamoring for it. We've got to produce a million if we're going to capitalize on this fad!"

"A million?" I asked. "Who's going to raise the money to pay for a million? Besides, that's too many games to start with."

"No, it isn't, Joe. I can sell a million just here in California. They are all going crazy for the idea," replied Howard.

"But, Howard, if they're going crazy, where are the orders?" I asked.

Howard proceeded to explain that the orders take a few weeks to issue and assured me that he was promised by everybody that he would have more orders than he could fill. He insisted that we didn't have time to waste and had to proceed with the production of the game if we wanted to capitalize on the Watergate news that was making headlines daily.

The game would sell for three dollars and cost distributors approximately $1.25. It cost us about 50¢ per game, so we stood to do quite well if we sold a million. But I still had my doubts.

I told Howard that I didn't want to risk any more of my capital. I had already paid out $5,000 to get the first batch of cards and boxes printed and didn't want to risk any more money until I knew for sure that the game really sold.

Howard suggested I contact my original JS&A investors and have them available for a sales presentation he would make in person. He would pass through Chicago on the way to our press conference in Washington and would talk to my group.

Howard came to my home and we held the presentation in my basement. I introduced Howard to my investors and he gave one of the most exciting presentations I have ever seen. It was so good that I, like my investors, ended up pledging money to produce a compromise 400,000 games without seeing one order and without talking to one buyer.

We all realized that Howard did not have a single penny in the deal, but his excuse was that the major effort he had to make was going to cost him a fortune in travel expenses. So nobody pressed the issue further. In fact, we advanced him all his travel expenses.

My investors had trusted me before and had received a good return on their investment. They felt that with dynamo Howard and my creative talent they couldn't lose.

Howard and I flew to Washington and held our press conference. The turnout was great. Reporters received copies of the game and photographed a few models actually playing it. The publicity made everything from the *Wall Street Journal* to *Time* magazine, and radio stations and newspapers were calling us from around the country for interviews.

My big job was production. Working around the clock, I got

not only the production organized but the packaging, the point-of-purchase displays, and the warehousing. It was a very difficult job with each project presenting its own problems.

Finally the games were in production and Howard arranged a tour for me. I was to appear on a number of TV shows in the Midwest while Howard would appear in California.

My first TV show was a disaster. The TV reporter started out the interview with the question, "Mr. Sugarman, how can you make fun of a serious thing like Watergate?"

I replied, "America needs to laugh at itself, to poke fun at itself. We need to laugh at a time like this."

But then, to my amazement, the reporter retaliated, "But surely Mr. Sugarman, making people laugh is one thing, but capitalizing on the misfortune of others is a disgrace. You say America needs someone poking fun at its politics and making money off the problems of others. No, Mr. Sugarman, you should be ashamed of yourself."

The reporter then started a tirade about the seriousness of the problem and urged the listeners to express their views on the telephone. Every one of them made me feel like crawling into a hole.

"I'm sorry," the reporter said. "I really feel it's my duty to tell it like it is."

I called Howard that night as I lay in bed wondering what went wrong. Howard still had no orders, but he said he would have some soon. He didn't sound too enthusiastic, but we were already committed and I knew Howard would come through.

My next interview was in a different city and also on TV. This reporter was a woman, considerably more friendly, and I was confident the interview would not be as bad as the last one. There were no phones in the studio for audience response. Prior to the show the reporter sympathized with my entrepreneurial spirit and was amazed at the short time it took to bring the product to market. But then the red light went on and the interview began:

"Mr. Sugarman, how could you make fun of a serious problem like Watergate?"

Not too worried, I answered, "America needs to laugh at itself. We need to make light of our serious problems. We must be able to poke fun at even our most serious misfortunes."

Suddenly, as if transformed into a witch, this friendly reporter proceeded to tear me and the game apart, live before a large St. Louis audience. I turned red, sweat forming on my brow, as I tried in vain to present my position. After the interview, this monster of a reporter turned back into that sympathetic lady. But it was too late.

I tried reaching Howard again that night. His wife answered the phone and I asked for Howard. She cupped the phone but I could hear her yell, "Howard, telephone."

Howard replied, "Tell him I'm not home," which I heard even through the cupped phone.

"What?" I said. "Tell Howard I just heard him say that and I better talk to him." But Howard refused to come to the phone. I knew something was wrong.

I had one interview left and I was determined to finish it and immediately return home to find out what was going on. The TV reporter sat me in a chair on a talk show set, the red light went on, and we were on the air.

"Mr. Sugarman, how could you make light of such a serious subject like Watergate?"

I looked at the reporter, paused for a moment and said, "I don't know. I'm embarrassed to be associated with this dumb game and I'm truly sorry I ever got involved in this thing in the first place. It's a stupid idea, and as far as I'm concerned, it was a big mistake."

The reporter looked at me dumbfounded. "But, Mr. Sugarman, don't you think Americans need to laugh at themselves, need to poke fun during serious times like these?" And he proceeded to try to convince me on the air that what I was doing was indeed good for all Americans.

When I got back to my office, it didn't take long before I realized Howard would no longer be reachable. I did manage to find out that none of the stores would handle the product because it was too controversial.

Once again I was stuck. But we tried to sell the game ourselves with very limited success. We did manage to sell 10,000 games to Canada. We exported 40,000 games to Australia. But in the United States, because we couldn't get distribution and because we couldn't even advertise the game in many magazines, we only sold about 5,000 games.

The 300,000-plus games took up a huge warehouse. I had lost, my investors had lost, and only Howard had come out ahead. Not only had he not put up any money, but his travel expenses had been far less than the advance we gave him.

I was so disappointed with the experience that I have not played the game since then. And, rather than transferring the games to the same warehouse where I kept my Batman credit cards, my Teeny Boppers and Mad records, I just gave them to my investors to liquidate as they saw fit.

I did keep three games. I thought that one of these days I could contribute my failures to the Smithsonian and I certainly wanted to include my latest example.

If I had just concentrated on JS&A and not gone off on another tangent, I would have been way ahead. Hadn't I learned my lessons by now?

15
Out of the Basement

I concentrated our advertising in the *Wall Street Journal*, running very large advertisements that extolled the virtues of my calculators with interesting pictures and extensive copy.

I'd rarely have less than 1,000 words in each ad, and I'd write the copy as if I were a salesman trying to sell my product to a very bright consumer. I respected the intelligence of my readers, so I avoided the stereotyped hype and advertising cliches. I tried to present as much consumer information as possible, and I presented this material with respect for my customers' judgment. This respect came across in my ads and consumers responded.

We also created the image of a very large company. Our ads were professional-looking, with no screaming headlines or exaggerated graphics. We consistently maintained this approach so that we soon had good recognition from *Journal* readers.

By concentrating on the *Wall Street Journal*, we also became one of their top ten advertisers—right up there with IBM, AT&T, and General Motors. In fact, examining the list of the top ten advertisers, you'd be convinced that JS&A was either a billion-dollar corporation like the rest of the list or, at a minimum, a company with a large corporate headquarters. Yet here we were, the four of us—Mary, Mary Ann, Wendy and I—operating out of the basement of my suburban home in Northbrook, Illinois.

In fact, Wendy wasn't even working full time. She had to look after April who at the time was not quite two years old and was always getting into trouble.

Chicago executives reading the *Wall Street Journal* would often call us on the phone and ask if they could come out to our corporate headquarters to pick up a calculator directly, instead of buying it through the mail.

Rather than lose the sale, we encouraged customers to visit us. Many times I would look out the living room window of my home and see a very well-dressed executive, sitting in his car, looking at the address in the advertisement and trying to convince himself that this home was the international headquarters of the huge JS&A empire.

I'd even see some customers sit there for five minutes trying to get up enough nerve to step out of their cars. When they eventually did, the typical customer, newspaper ad in hand, would walk up to the front door and ring the bell. Wendy, who would be carrying April, would answer the door and April usually chose this time to be screaming her lungs out.

Embarrassed and disoriented, our customers would walk down the stairs to the basement and I would end up selling them a calculator. And they never failed to leave our home quite surprised. They expected, at a minimum, a skyscraper, and they saw a basement. They expected a huge organization and they saw four people and a screaming baby.

And they talked about it when they got back to their corporate worlds. As the word spread, people were soon visiting us out of curiosity, and by mid-1973 there was so much traffic in our basement that we couldn't get much work done. Some of our neighbors were beginning to wonder what was going on, since the front of our house was turning into a parking lot.

There were also people who stopped by before they went to work—some at 6:30 in the morning. Wendy and I didn't appreciate that. Then there were those customers who would stop by at night—sometimes as late at 10:30. Wendy and I didn't like that either. And of course, there was the constant fear that one of our customers was really a professional burglar casing the place for a robbery.

As the traffic grew and the inconvenience mounted, I decided it was time to find a new facility. Just a few blocks away from my home, George Olson, a local real estate man, had converted an old gas station into a modest one-story office building.

The building had a thousand square feet, which seemed huge when compared to our basement, which was half the size. And we had to pay rent—six hundred dollars—which seemed like a frightening burden, especially since we had to sign a three-year lease.

I had never had overhead and six hundred dollars a month really bothered me. I feared that my little business would burst its bubble and I'd be stuck with the rent if, one day, times got rough.

But on January 1, 1974, JS&A moved its entire operation from the basement of my home to the corner of Sanders and Dundee roads in Northbrook. I now had overhead and the realization that I had a business with enough space to grow.

16
The Big Jump

Within a few months after we moved into our new offices I hit with a very successful ad that I felt was worth advertising nationally in hundreds of other magazines and newspapers. The response was so strong that we increased our staff from two people to fifteen and quickly grew out of our thousand-square-foot space.

The ad that proved so successful was for a liquid crystal calculator, one of the first on the market, called the Data King 800. It had great features and a good price, and we presented it in a very exciting and forceful manner. But what really made it a big seller was a small paragraph that appeared in the ad:

"Want to exchange your old, outdated calculator for the Data King 800 without losing too much money? We've got a way. After you are absolutely satisfied with your Data King 800, send us your outdated unit. JS&A will then send it to a deserving school, nonprofit organization, or charitable institution which in turn will send you a letter of appreciation and a certificate acknowledging your contribution. Then use that contribution as a legitimate deduction on your income tax return. You'll be helping somebody in need, while justifying the purchase of the latest calculator technology."

People were so impressed with the service we were providing those needy institutions that they responded in great numbers. Not only did we do well on the campaign, but we helped a number of needy institutions that really appreciated our efforts.

The program netted us close to one half million dollars from that single advertisement and represented more money than I thought I'd ever see in my lifetime. That single advertisement changed the entire nature of our business and we now had the staff and the capital to expand and grow.

Our WATS lines had increased from two to six and our cramped operation looked exactly like a bookie joint if you happened to be stopping by to purchase a calculator.

We were so jammed that we knew we had to find newer quarters—a place that gave us an opportunity to operate comfortably and also a place that would permit us to grow if we needed more space.

I found a new building in the industrial park a few miles from my home and moved in my fifteen employees and all our furniture. The 6,000-square-foot facility seemed huge, but it didn't take me long to fill it up. I bought the piece of property next to the office site and built a warehouse, and we used our old office as a retail showroom for the remainder of our lease.

17
Famous JS&A Customers

One of the many benefits of running a well-known national mail order company is the very famous clientele that you develop throughout the years.

When my secretary buzzes me to tell me that Robert Redford is on the phone or Spiro Agnew wants to talk to me, it no longer seems unusual.

We have many famous customers, including country and western singers, movie stars, comedians, politicians, newscasters, TV personalities, and many stars of the past.

One of the most exciting orders I received came in 1976. As I passed near the mail desk, one of the young ladies called out to me, "Mr. Sugarman, look who just ordered from us."

I looked at the order and it was from Frank Sinatra. Sinatra had sent us a check accompanied by a letter ordering one of our products.

That very day I was expecting two friends I hadn't seen for a long time. I really wanted to impress them, so I borrowed the Sinatra check and letter.

To understand why I wanted to impress them, you'd have to understand my friends. They were the type of guys who always had to be one up on you.

If you bought a new car, they would always talk about a faster, better, or more expensive version of the same model that one of their friends owned. I can remember telling them one year that my next-door neighbor had just installed an underground sprinkling system only to have one of them blurt out, "I know somebody who has a waterfall."

"Who cares?" I would always think, but I could never come up with any real rebuttal to their nonsense.

The Sinatra order, however, gave me a great idea for a practical joke. I was sure my friends would be impressed with my new offices, but I knew they wouldn't admit it. What I wanted to do was really shock them so they couldn't come up with their usual, "That's nothing, Joe," routine.

So I told Mary Stanke to buzz me three minutes after they entered my office and tell me over the intercom, "Mr. Sugarman, Frank Sinatra is on the phone and he'd like to talk to you." Meanwhile, I placed the Sinatra order in the center of a pile of other papers at the side of my desk.

True to form, my friends sat down in front of my desk and proceeded to be unimpressed with our offices or the level of success I had achieved.

"Joe, you should see the other offices I just visited yesterday," said one of them in an effort to minimize his impression of our place.

Suddenly, Mary buzzed me on the intercom, "Mr. Sugarman, Frank Sinatra is on the phone and he'd like to talk to you."

I reached for the intercom, "Mary, tell Frank that we got his order and we'll get it out as quickly as possible. Also, tell him I'm in a conference and I can't talk to him right now."

The expressions on my friends' faces were a real delight. Their mouths hung open as they stared in disbelief. Finally one of them waved his hands vehemently and said, "Joe, talk to him; please talk to him."

"No, I won't," I said. "You're more important to me than Frank Sinatra."

It didn't take more than a few seconds after that comment for one of my friends to say, "Aw, Joe, that wasn't Frank Sinatra; you're playing a practical joke on us."

"Just one second," I retorted indignantly. I then started searching through my stack of papers looking for the Sinatra order and taking my time in the process.

Finally, I found the order and the check and flipped it to the other side of my desk as if almost insulted that they would accuse me of trying to deceive them. "Here, take a look."

They examined the letter and the check and noted the current date and sat back once again in disbelief. My practical joke had totally disarmed them. There was nothing they could say to top the mere thought that they were more important to me than Frank Sinatra.

Just before they left, I told them the truth and we all had a good laugh. And the story normally would have ended there except for an episode that took place the following day at exactly the same time.

I was sitting in my office when Mary Stanke buzzed me on the intercom, "Mr. Sugarman, Marlon Brando is on the phone and he'd like to talk to you."

I reached for the intercom and replied, "Mary, my friends are gone."

Indeed, it was Marlon Brando. And we talked for about half an hour about a few of the products we were marketing.

Even when I meet some of these personalities in person I often discover that they've been buying our products for years.

I had the opportunity to meet Pat Boone at his home one day, only to discover that the watch he was wearing was ours.

Politicians, top corporate executives, and international states-men buy our products. And as I mentioned in the beginning of this chapter, it is not surprising to be buzzed on my intercom and hear the name of a famous personality.

The mail order business is one of the few businesses that could cater to such an impressive list of customers. And it certainly adds a degree of excitement to our order-takers' lives.

18
The Growth Continues

JS&A grew and grew. I continued to do all the copywriting, as I always did. I'd set the headlines on my photo typositor and Wendy would set the body type on our IBM composer.

While in the new building I purchased a new computer, computerized microfilm systems, and every conceivable modern piece of space-age office equipment to make our operation more efficient.

And we continued attracting the most advanced products and building our success and reputation in the process.

Despite our success, I always made it a point to treat all our suppliers and friends with the same respect I had always had for them. Sucess did not change us. We constantly strived to provide good service and maintain a high degree of honesty and integrity.

One of the reasons for the outstanding success of my business was the effort expended by each one of my employees. They learned to respond to every problem by turning that problem into an opportunity to show our customers how we cared.

Mary Stanke is the most brilliant example of a dedicated employee. Trained as a secretary, she worked for Chrysler Corporation for a few years. She then retired to raise her two daughters while her husband handsomely supported his family as a foreman at a Chicago printing company, Rogers Park Press.

When Mary first started she was earning $3.25 an hour. Today she has become the general manager of JS&A, executive vice-president, and makes a handsome salary—quite an achievement for a secretary.

Her rise through JS&A was not surprising. She worked whatever hours were necessary to get the job done. She was honest, so I could trust her to look after the books and my interests, and she made sure the business ran smoothly even while I was out of town. Actually, it ran better when I was out of town.

What was even more remarkable was how she was able to dedicate herself to her job and yet raise her two children, feed her family, and be a good housewife as well.

Mary has always called me Mr. Sugarman. It was her way of formally expressing the respect she had for the position I held and the job that I had done.

Mary also looked after my interests. She warned me about a few people I should have avoided and was always right. She adapted to every new level of growth, learning new skills and creating new systems. If Wendy was the secret to my bouncing back, it was another woman, Mary Stanke, who was the secret to my successful bounce upward.

Mary never had to ask me for a raise. I have always paid her more than she expected and supported her decisions, which often were exactly those that I would make anyway.

Today all I need to do for JS&A is provide a direction for the company, select the products that Mary's staff prescreens, and then write the ads. She does the rest and does it well.

Building JS&A was not easy but, with the support of Mary

and a staff that followed her example, it is not surprising that JS&A grew.

For every product we advertised we learned that regardless of how we prepared, something always went wrong.

Either we were back-ordered on a product or it arrived defective and we had to return entire shipments. Some of our suppliers went bankrupt and many broke promises to us, causing us to look bad to our customers. The problems associated with our successes were endless with countless disappointments and a stream of unexpected setbacks. But we never gave up and always looked at the yearly balance sheet of our company and saw how we grew an average of 40 percent a year, year after year.

We answered all our correspondence, dealt with customers honestly, and treated every complaint as if it came from a next-door neighbor. My early experiences taught me how important service was in building a company.

We weren't perfect and occasionally we made mistakes, but whenever we did, we admitted it and corrected it in a responsible and prompt manner.

I also learned that whenever I dealt with honest suppliers, they responded responsibly whenever problems arose. Whenever I dealt with dishonest suppliers, they disappeared when problems arose. Problems were always a fact of business life, but I learned quickly how to choose a product—first choose an honest supplier.

JS&A had grown into a highly respected small business with sales of twelve million dollars, a staff of sixty people, and a reputation of service and honesty in all its dealings.

By the summer of 1978, the company was prepared to launch its biggest advertising drive in its continued growth. We were on the way to introducing the most exciting new products in our young history, with a new computer software program and a series of new innovations that would catapult us toward becoming a fifty-million-dollar-a-year company. The years of hard work were really starting to bear fruit.

19
My Mail Order Lessons

The mail order business was like a rapid series of experiences, each with its own lessons and each lesson with its own message.

Instead of an isolated Batman experience or a once-in-a-lifetime Teeny Bopper fiasco—I had had these failure experiences almost one after another. True, I was occasionally lucky, and one of my ads was successful. And true, I discovered through these successes valuable insights and philosophies. The more meaningful experiences, however, came from my failures, for it was those painful failures that taught me the most.

When I started in business, my ad successes were about eight to two. For every eight failures, there seemed always to be two advertisements that were successful enough to make up for the eight that weren't. And the eight that weren't gave me a real education.

I learned a great deal about people. I could tell within a few moments of meeting someone whether I was going to be success-

ful in working with them. Through all my failures I discovered
that certain actions by my suppliers and the people I did
business with were going to lead inevitably to these suppliers'
success or failure.

After a few years in business, I could predict who was going
to be around and succeed and who was going to fail. And so
when a supplier tried to cheat me, although I got upset, I
absolutely knew that his dishonesty would eventually lead to his
failure.

Once I realized the subtle things that literally forced people to
succeed or fail, I started to develop a set of philosophies and
directed myself using these philosophies.

So accurate are these philosophies that I can often predict the
outcome of my actions even though the outcome is contrary to
what everybody would expect.

My success rate with advertisements still runs about eight to
two, but now there are eight successes against two losers. I'm
still quite proud of the losers. They're all great lessons that make
me even better at what I do.

It recently took two failures with telephone products before I
hit with one telephone that really sold. But from the two losses
and the one winner, I learned how to sell telephones.

The mail order industry and the rapid sequence of failures
and successes were a proving ground for my Success Force
philosophies. Sure, I had laid the groundwork before I had run
my first advertisement, but it was my business experiences that
confirmed these philosophies.

The Success Forces have become so important to me that I
have learned to follow them closely, for I know that I will
continue to succeed despite myself if I follow them.

The Success Force philosophy is not something you can feel,
see, or measure. It nevertheless is a real force that exerts an
energy that will either force you toward success or force you
toward failure.

Simply knowing those forces will be an excellent starting
point. Then you can observe the results when you follow the

force versus those when you don't. Only then can you prove to yourself how effective my Success Forces really are.

In the following section I will describe my Success Forces in detail. The first section of this book was designed to give you an insight into the evolution of Joe Sugarman—of the failures that taught me what didn't work and the successes that taught me what did.

This next section will present the very basic forces that I am convinced will work for anyone. They are not complicated. In fact, they are rather basic—but they are incredibly powerful if you'll believe in and use them.

SECTION II

Introduction

The Theory of Success Forces

I am convinced that for every action you take a force is created—and that this force will either steer or force you toward success or toward failure.

I am also convinced that there are six very important Success Forces that, if understood, will bring you success—often despite yourself.

My very prosperous Chinese and Japanese friends have a philosophy that seems to tie in very closely with mine. They feel that there are existing forces in nature that guide your destiny. If you are honest and honorable and follow the natural direction to which these forces point you, you will succeed.

These forces aren't meant to be spiritual or mystical, but rather the very subtle effects of your actions. If you find it hard to visualize the concept of Success Forces, picture a beam scale with two trays on each side balanced at a point in the center. Put weight on one side and it is forced down while the other side

111

is forced up. Add enough weight on the side that's high and it will eventually sink below the other side. So it is with Success Forces. Take actions that add force to the success side of your scale and you create a force that brings success. Take actions that result in the opposite—Failure Forces—and the results are just the opposite.

What makes me an authority on success? That's why I included a biographical sketch of my life in the first part of this book. I have been on both sides of the scale enough times to know what works and what doesn't. If all I knew was success, I doubt I would have been able to discover the real Success Forces and then personally witness them working.

Always Be Honest

Honesty is the strongest and most powerful Success Force.

Now, you might have expected something more dramatic than honesty to lead off this section of my book, but if you'll follow my logic, you'll discover just how powerful honesty as a Success Force really is, and then we can build from there.

First, let's discuss the misconceptions. Some people feel that in business, to come out on top, you've sometimes got to lie, cheat, and bribe. And you might have thought that the poor, naive, honest person doing business with someone who is unscrupulous is really at a disadvantage. These are misconceptions.

Honesty will put you right on top. No matter whom you confront, no matter what situation you find yourself in, honesty does work. And it works, as you will see, so effectively that your whole perception of dishonesty is bound to change.

In business, whenever I see anybody do anything dishonest, I tell my staff, "Don't worry, they won't be around very long." I

113

say this with such confidence that Mary Stanke once asked me why I was so positive.

I couldn't tell her why, but I told her to keep an eye on three companies and two individuals and track their paths. "See where they go and how quickly they fail."

One by one, she tracked them and they each followed my predictions. How could I predict the future in this regard so accurately?

I can remember an experience with a non-profit organization's magazine in 1978. We had been advertising in this fraternal magazine for almost five years and we were scheduled for a new digital watch advertisement in their November issue.

At the last minute the magazine's publisher called Mary Stanke and canceled us out of the issue. I don't usually work personally with the magazines we place ads in, but I felt I needed an explanation. What went wrong?

So I called the publisher, whom I had known for five years, but I couldn't get an explanation from him that made sense. He couldn't give me any straight answers. He also stopped sending us free issues of his magazine and took us off his mailing list completely.

It wasn't until that issue finally came out that we saw why. One of our competitors was running a digital watch ad in that issue and on the same page we had planned to run our advertisement.

Was the publisher bribed to cancel our ad and put our competitor's ad in? I don't know. I did know that the advertiser who had taken our position had a bad reputation. Was I upset? Not at all. It was an indication to me that both the advertiser and the magazine were dishonest and would eventually pay their dues. As it happened, the advertiser eventually went bankrupt, leaving the magazine holding the bag for a great deal of money. We stopped advertising in the publication, which deprived the magazine of at least $100,000 in advertising revenue. And we discovered a few new fraternal magazines that worked very well for us—ones we might not have discovered had it not been for the rejection we got from the magazine that treated us so badly.

I have observed enough dishonesty to know that there is a very strong failure force associated with dishonesty. More important, however, is that there is a very powerful Success Force created by honesty. Without a doubt, the more honest you are, the more successful you will ultimately become.

Let's acknowledge a few facts about honesty. First, it's relative. What is honest to you might not be to somebody else. And then there's the degree of honesty to be considered. Honesty to an extreme may be both impractical and lacking in common sense. Driving ten miles to return a nickel to a customer you overcharged might be impractical and ludicrous, even though it is honest.

Honesty, in its relative sense, is judged strictly by the eyes of the beholder. It would be ludicrous to drive ten miles to return a nickel overcharge. But what amount, if any, would cause *you* to drive the ten miles?

Each time you are honest and conduct yourself with honesty, a Success Force will drive you toward greater success. Each time you lie, even with a little white lie, there are strong forces pushing you toward failure.

With this in mind, each time you have a choice to be honest or dishonest and you choose to be honest, your chances of success are greater.

The force may not work right away. As a matter of fact, it may not show up for months. It may be very painful to tell the truth, and you may even question how telling the truth in a painful situation will result in your eventual success. But it will.

The more painful it is to tell the truth, the greater the Success Force you create. How do you get this Success Force to work for you and how do you know if it does indeed work? That will come from your own personal experiences. The simple fact that you are aware of honesty as a powerful Success Force will help you discover this important phenomenon.

I will cite just a few observations that I have made, although they are not as convincing as having you discover for yourself just how effective honesty can really be in bringing you success.

At JS&A I've always insisted on honesty as our number one policy. We treat our customers with respect and we have a cardinal rule that all questions, when asked, are answered honestly.

We also conduct our business relationships with honesty. If we order 1,000 calculators and the manufacturer ships us 1,020 by mistake and bills us for only 1,000, we let him know and pay for the 20 extra pieces or return them.

No employee can be fired for telling the truth at JS&A—no matter how embarrassing. All of our advertising is first checked by the manufacturers and then by our lawyers. Every statement is checked thoroughly. If there's an exaggeration, it's toned down to reflect the truth. Every fact must be accurate. But if by chance we do make a mistake in an advertising claim, we always admit it, correct the mistake, and often advise our customers.

If one of our customers is treated poorly and it's our fault, we admit it and try to correct the matter to the fair and just satisfaction of the customer. We also try to hire very honest people.

The popular misconception that to be successful in business you've got to be dishonest—or at least a little dishonest—is not true. I don't believe it. Sure, I've known dishonest people in business. Pretty soon people find out about them. Eventually everything comes back to hit you square in the face.

Quite often I've known people who are willing to swing a dishonest deal, make a fast buck and disappear. They never really make it, despite what you hear. In all my experience in business, every dishonest businessman is eventually found out and travels under a dark cloud. He doesn't see the cloud, but everybody he deals with does.

Sure, the dishonest individual makes a fast buck, but he pays for it over and over again in the long run. Remember, he's constantly creating negative forces—Failure Forces—the opposite of Success Forces.

There are indeed some people who are dishonest and seem to

get away with it. But do they? I know of a rip-off artist who cheated thousands of consumers and supposedly got away with it, making millions of dollars and driving around in a Rolls Royce.

But that's from the outside. His family life failed, he had major health problems, and he experienced real heartbreaks and failures. I contend that dishonesty will create a failure force that often manifests itself in other ways—often not apparent to the outside observer.

But if you're in business and you agree that honesty is the best policy, how do you avoid being "taken" and still keep this powerful force working in your favor? What is the key?

The key is to protect yourself. By protecting yourself, I mean dealing with honest people to start with. When you deal with honest people, chances are you'll work better together and you'll have trust in each other. You'll spend less time worrying about each other's motives and more time on how you can both succeed. There will be less time-consuming politics, and you'll feel free to move on the other person's word when delay can mean a lost opportunity.

When you deal with honest people, it is a great pleasure and it is enjoyable; great things get accomplished in a very short period of time. Contrast this with a dishonest relationship. You're constantly cautious, you're spending more time protecting yourself than you are devoting to your business. You sign detailed contracts that in a dishonest relationship don't mean much anyway.

That's not to say you don't sign contracts with people you feel are honest. Quite the contrary. An honest person may be very honest, but he may have a poor memory. Sign contracts or at least exchange letters. Do something to document your decisions and understandings.

When I first meet somebody, I try to find out if they're honest. If I feel they are honest and I can trust them, we can develop a good business relationship. That's how I pick some of my products. I first pick the people.

When a manufacturer presents a product to me at JS&A it

doesn't take too long before I discover whether the guy is lying to me. When this happens, his chances of having me market his product are very slim.

A gentleman who once presented me with a product volunteered to me the price he was allegedly paying for it from the Far East. It just so happened I knew what that particular product costs from the Far East, and exactly what he was paying for it, as a result of a unique coincidence.

Now, you might say, "Well, that's the way you do business. You use a little white lie every once in a while."

Not true. I would rather he had said nothing than lie to me. How do I know if his next statement will be true? If he volunteers a dishonest statement, how can I rely on any answer he'd give to my questions?

I was very reluctant to deal with this man. Deep inside I really didn't want to do business with him. If he had been honest, he could have walked away with a sale for his product. But he walked away with nothing, and the funny part is that he doesn't know why.

There are so many ways to distinguish the phonies from the honest individuals. Just ask enough questions and they'll dig themselves into a hole.

A very good acquaintance of mine, an author and lecturer, once had dinner with me and I told him about a few speeches I had given and asked his advice on how to give a better speech.

He told me the key ingredients of preparing and giving a speech—what it should contain, how it should be presented. He gave me the reasoning and the logic behind his views, and after I finished dinner I really felt I had learned a great deal.

There is an interesting relationship between how you give a speech and how I had been writing my ads. In fact, the rules are parallel. So I prepared my next speech along the lines of my successful advertisements. My next two speeches were sensational. In a short time I had mastered the art and I was invited to give a keynote speech before 500 people at the Southern California Direct Marketing Convention in Los Angeles. The speech turned out to be fantastic and the audience gave me a standing ovation.

I had the speech taped and sent the tape recording with great pride and enthusiasm to my friend and advisor for his opinion. About a week later I called him, anxious to hear his reaction to my speech. "Joe, I think you were too vain in your talk; you should be more modest. Your accomplishments are nice to hear about, but I think you're better off not highlighting them yourself," he said.

It came as a total shock. His criticism of my speech and the tape I had sent him were not one and the same. "Are you sure you heard the tape?" I asked him.

"Of course I did," he said.

"Because it doesn't sound like the same one I gave you," I replied.

"Well, Joe, I'll listen to it again."

It was rather obvious to me that he hadn't heard the tape. In my speech I had talked primarily of my failures—not of my successes. And I had presented my talk with great humility, not the vanity my advisor said I had expressed. But, I waited, and a few days later he called back.

"Joe, you were sensational. I've never heard a more interesting, inspirational speech in my life. You have a really bright future ahead of you if you just want to be a public speaker."

It was obvious to me he indeed had not heard the tape the first time. Suddenly his future advice and comments had to be weighed. If he used a white lie to avoid an embarrassing situation, how would he respond to other situations?

In his position, I would have been honest and said that I hadn't had the opportunity to review the tape. If someone calls me and asks me if I have done something and it is extremely embarrassing to admit that I have not, I admit it regardless of the consequences.

Honesty has to be worked at. It's not easy, because sometimes it seems that the easiest thing is to tell a little white lie to avoid embarrassment. But don't do it. Every lie brings into existence a negative failure force and every honest answer a positive Success Force.

Another mail order entrepreneur recently wrote a book on how to make a million in mail order. In the book he made a few statements that were not truthful. One statement credited him with being the first to introduce the pocket calculator. Since I was intimately involved with the introduction of the pocket calculator and the companies and personalities at the time, and knew the entire situation, I was able to recognize his comments as being untruthful. His entire book became meaningless to me. How could I trust his book, his advice, or anything else? And knowing the mail order business as I do, it wasn't long before I discovered more untrue statements in his book. I know that I won't deal with this man in the future and I am convinced that his lies create a negative failure force.

Now, I'm not perfect either. I have made statements that have come back and hit me like a boomerang.

Even though I work at being honest, I do slip. It's human to err, but I've also seen these slips come back and haunt me with a negative failure force that makes me regret any dishonesty— even a white lie.

If you can use honesty as your guiding philosophy, you'll be amazed at how powerful it is. I find that honesty is a strong and effective force in advertising. I always bring up a negative feature of a product and I avoid exaggerating any of the positive features of whatever I sell. My customers sense this honesty and know they are dealing with an honest company, and they therefore respond.

Whenever I try to cover up a small flaw or fault in a product, it haunts me, and I've never succeeded. Whenever I have been frank and honest, I've been my most successful.

Honesty is a very powerful force. It may be the rougher road to take, it may be a little embarrassing at times, but if you use honesty as the cornerstone of the Success Force philosophy, you'll never go wrong.

Cherish Your Failures

One of the most powerful Success Forces is failure. Every time you fail you create a positive force for success.

To explain how this force works, let's examine a baby when he takes his first steps. What happens? He falls. So he tries and tries again. Finally, after many failures, the little toddler starts to walk. Wobbly at first, but he is walking.

The baby at first failed to walk, but each time he fell, he learned something. From all his failures, he was able to learn enough to balance himself and walk without falling.

I contend that this process works throughout one's entire life. We learn from our failures. Pile up enough failures and success is a sure bet. But most of us don't like failure. In fact, we avoid it at all costs, even if it means missing out on an opportunity.

I am firmly convinced that failure is such a powerful Success Force that it gives me the reassurance to try almost anything, for I know that even if I fail, it will create a force for success later.

When I was twenty years old, and working in New York on Spectra '59, I had already experienced many failures in life. I had a philosophy in 1959 that I continue to believe in.

Every time I failed, I said to myself, "Well, I'll put it in my back pocket and one of these days when I need it, I'll reach in and take it out." I meant, of course, the lesson that I had learned. In today's computer society, I might have simply said that I was "programming my computer and storing the data."

The Chinese have a theory which they express about failure and success. Simply stated, it says that no matter what course of action you take, whether you succeed or fail, it is more important that you at least act in an attempt to succeed or fail. They believe that if you take action, in the long run you will succeed regardless of how many times you fail. They view "not taking action" as a much bigger disgrace than failing.

Certainly among the most interesting aspects of my life is how many times I have failed. Whenever I give a speech, I always start off with a story about a few failures I've had that might interest the audience.

Then I tell my audience, "I'm here today not because I'm a huge success but because I have probably failed more times than anybody in this room. But from all of these failures, I have learned things and from the things that I've learned, I have been able to succeed."

I've piled up so many failures in my life that I could fill several volumes with the stories. But I discovered that from each failure I always learned something that I could place in my "back pocket" and use later in some other form.

If my premise is correct, it's just a matter of time until those failures start to add up and create a tremendous force to succeed. But there's a problem. Who likes to fail?

Most of us go through life with big egos and try to avoid failure. However, you must realize that failure is one of the Success Forces, and that to get the "opportunity" to fail is also to be able to increase your opportunity for success in the future.

I am supposedly an expert at picking products to market through my company. Yet the truth is that every product I thought was going to be a huge success turned out average at best, and many products I thought were average or below turned out to be super winners. And the story is the same for all my endeavors. Every time I thought I was on the way to great success I was disappointed, and every time I least expected it I scored big.

There's an interesting conclusion here. If all I ever did was attempt those projects I was convinced were sure winners, I would have achieved only average success. It was my acceptance of possible failure that let me attempt those seemingly average or losing opportunities that eventually led to great success.

If you then realize that failure is indeed a force—more powerful than success—then you'll understand one of the truly powerful forces that works in your favor each time you experience it.

But there's a key. Just as "protect yourself" was the key to honesty, the key to failure is to "bounce back." Look at the failure as a learning experience. Learn from your failure those things that are worth putting in your back pocket and then tackle the next project.

Learning from your failures creates a great Success Force. So realize quickly the lessons learned, realize that failure isn't so bad after all, and above all—bounce back.

The problem with most people is that they don't learn from their failures or they give up. Failure is only as powerful as what you get out of it. By understanding just how powerful it can be, and accepting it as a Success Force, you will gain more courage to attempt new and different things.

Many of the success books talk about persistence as the ultimate way to achieve success. Isn't persistence really a way of saying, "I've failed but I know why I failed; I've learned something new, and I must continue until I succeed."

Not many people are willing to give failure a second opportunity. They fail once and it's all over. The bitter pill of failure—

often combined with embarrassment and deflated egos—is more than most people can handle.

I have failed so many times, even during my supposedly successful years with JS&A, that I am convinced of the power and the impact failure has as one of the Success Forces.

I'm not suggesting that if you want to go out and achieve success, you should go out and try to fail. I am saying that you should attempt things in life with the attitude that *if you fail*, you should consider it a blessing—a Success Force that later will let you succeed beyond your wildest imagination.

To fail and bounce back requires a lot of resilience. I don't want to give you the impression that failure was a pleasure for me. It wasn't; it was quite painful. I can remember working for a solid year only to lose every penny I owned in a bad deal or in a promotion that didn't work. Remember my Batman credit card, my Teeny Bopper promotion and my Watergate game—all painful and hard lessons? But I never gave up and I always bounced back.

My failures weren't pleasant and I certainly wouldn't want to relive those days. I doubt anybody relishes those kinds of memories. But I do owe my present success to those earlier failures, the things I learned, and the positive Success Forces they created.

If you're willing to accept failure and learn from it, if you're willing to consider failure as a blessing in disguise and bounce back, you've got the potential of harnessing one of the most powerful Success Forces.

Relish Your Problems

A powerful Success Force can be created by the way you view a problem.

Problems, as well as failures, are negative things. But problems have a hidden ingredient that makes them very effective in creating a Success Force. The word is "opportunity."

Each problem has hidden in it an opportunity so powerful that it literally dwarfs the problem. The greatest success stories were created by people who recognized a problem and turned it into an opportunity.

If you can program yourself to view every problem as an opportunity, can you imagine what a powerful force you can apply to your life?

When the digital watch first came out, it had a high defect rate. At JS&A we looked at this problem as an opportunity to prove to our customers what a good company we are.

We gave customers loaner watches while we repaired their

defective ones. We paid them their postage costs for mailing their watches to us.

We soon had many compliments on our concept. We received letters from customers who told us that they were so amazed at the service they received that they told their friends about it and their friends bought watches from us too. One man reported that he was personally responsible for the sale of a dozen watches, while another had convinced his entire company of the value we provided with our warranty. His company orders watches from us to this day.

We turned a real problem into an opportunity to prove our commitment to service to our customers, and the results were quite successful.

The digital watch story is only one example of how we took problems and turned them into opportunities. Whenever you have a problem, the best thing to say to yourself is, "Okay, I've got a problem but hidden in there is an opportunity. Where is it, and what is it?

Sometimes you can't see it. It's well hidden. Other times, simply looking for the opportunity forces one to pop out. Even the more difficult-to-find opportunities, those that you may not be able to see right away, pop up if you work at it long enough.

There is no exception to this rule. It works as surely as the other Success Forces. Let the problem consume you and you create a failure force. But take that problem, turn it around by finding the opportunity, and you create a Success Force.

Many things in life are similar to the problems-opportunity relationship. When found in the ground a diamond may resemble a piece of coal—full of black carbon. But that ugly stone—when polished, cut, and placed in a setting—becomes the most beautiful gem in the world.

Look at how you take problems and turn them into opportunities as in the coal-diamond example. Your opportunities are camouflaged, just like the diamond. Spend a little time polishing, or even looking at your problem in a different way, and you'll be amazed at how the opportunities pop up.

I'd like to offer a few suggestions on how to help you find that opportunity in your next problem. First, say to yourself that there is an opportunity. Without conviction you'll never find it.

Second, restate the problem. Often just stating it differently will open up an entire new perspective that will produce a whole list of opportunities. Let me give you a little lesson in restating a problem.

Let's take the digital watch example. We could have stated the problem very simply by saying, "Providing service for digital watches is a problem."

Or, we may say, "Consumers are upset with the quality of digital watches and they are concerned about service."

Both of the above state the problem quite clearly and are accurate statements. However, let's restate our problem a little differently: "What can JS&A do to remove the problem of digital watch service?" Or, maybe, "What would our customers appreciate about our servicing their defective watches?"

Already you see that by simply restating the problem, you get a totally different perspective. We went from a problem and then took it full circle to viewing the problem from the customer's perspective. That is exactly how we turned the service program into an opportunity. We restated the problem and, simply by doing that, we got a different perspective that we later developed into our watch service program.

Looking at problems from different perspectives and restating a problem from a different viewpoint often leads to discovering the opportunity present in every problem. With a little practice and a positive attitude, you'll always find that opportunity. It's always there.

Looking at your problems as just problems will bring you failure. Looking at your problems as opportunities will create a powerful Success Force.

Concentrate Your Powers

If you've ever taken a magnifying glass on a sunny day and focused the concentrated beam of the sun on a piece of paper, you know the power of concentration. The paper will ignite in a matter of seconds. Without the ability to concentrate the sun's rays, the paper would never burn.

The same concept can also be described as one of my Success Forces. By zeroing in on a few targets and concentrating your efforts, you create tremendous forces that act to accelerate success.

Whenever I have concentrated on my business, it has brought me success. Whenever I go off on a tangent, I have failed. If you already understand how I view failure, you can best understand the concept of concentration.

One of my suppliers, Texas Instruments, has found that at the beginning stages of a project, production is low and the cost per unit is high. As they learn from their failures, the productivity

128

is increased. This process follows a curve that Texas Instruments has been able to plot and calls "The Learning Curve."

In life we follow the same type of curve in all our endeavors. By concentrating solidly on one area, you eventually learn from your mistakes, and as you learn, your productivity increases. The more you concentrate, the more confined an area you work in, the less chance of failure.

Go off on a tangent and what happens? You enter a brand new learning curve. You make an entirely new series of mistakes and you experience a whole new series of failures.

Something else happens when you go off on a tangent. You divert your attention from your area of prime effectiveness. You lose on two counts.

By concentrating on a specific area and avoiding tangents, you create tremendous Success Forces. The more you concentrate, the better your chances of success. In my business, I started out by concentrating only in micro-electronic products. I concentrated my early advertising campaigns in the *Wall Street Journal*. I concentrated on big ads. I concentrated with the same format for my advertising. The more I found ways to concentrate myself, the easier success came.

Every time I took a departure, or went off on a tangent, I paid the consequences. While successfully concentrating my efforts with JS&A, I was encouraged to take my first tangent with my Watergate game. Not only did I have to learn an entirely new business, but I was diverted from my very highly productive activity with JS&A. The only redeeming value in the whole Watergate tangent was that I learned from the failure (Success Force Two), but I would have rather concentrated on my business.

Just as there is a secret to the Success Forces of honesty and failure there is also a secret to concentration. "Don't go off on tangents." Tangents are dangerous. I learned how dangerous they are when I saw my father operate his business. He had a beautiful process camera manufacturing operation. He manufactured the cameras that printers used to produce plates, but as he succeeded, he thought he could build his empire by importing products from overseas, and then by owning manufacturing facilities overseas. He soon overextended himself and ended up almost going under.

All his competitors in the camera business concentrated on making cameras and they prospered and grew. My dad's business floundered. I always felt that if my dad had concentrated on his camera business, he could have been number one and very prosperous today. I learned from my father. I learned what not to do. I learned what happens when you go off on tangents.

Decide how many things you can concentrate on and discipline yourself not to go off on tangents. You'll then discover that concentration is a powerful Success Force.

Do It Differently

If you are one of those who read JS&A's advertisements, you might have observed a number of companies who run mail order ads that look very similar to ours. They use the same type faces, the same layout and the same photographic style that we do.

It would seem logical that if anyone were trying to break into the mail order business, the first thing he or she would do is to try to duplicate our approach, copy our product selection, and look like us.

Yet, I believe that every element you copy is a failure force. And every time you innovate or do something different, you create a very powerful Success Force. The secret, therefore, is "don't copy."

Some of my biggest failures occurred when I simply tried to copy someone else's success and not innovate on my own. Copying has two strikes against it. In the first place there's my First Law of Confusion, which states that "Nothing will happen as it

131

should." Throughout my life, every concept I thought was going to turn out to be a huge success ended in failure, in great disappointment, or at best, in a slight success. And many marginal-appearing concepts turned out to be my real success stories.

Copying a success follows my law. The success has the absolute appearance of success and therefore its chances of success are quite slim.

The second strike against copying is my Second Law of Confusion, which states, "Every success is comprised of several obvious elements and several billion not so obvious ones." The point is that in order to come near duplicating a success, you've got to duplicate its elements, the majority of which you are not aware of. But even if you were successful, the most difficult element to copy is timing.

How can you possibly duplicate a time in space—a time when all other elements of the success were in just the right position to achieve success? Every time I have copied, I have failed. Every time I have innovated, I have, on the average, done quite well. The more innovation, the greater the success.

During my days of handling advertising for the Schuss Mountain Ski Resort, a rock group that had played for me at Frank Bond's on a few occasions was to perform near the resort in nearby Traverse City. Traverse City had a beautiful 3,000-seat auditorium and had a small college that often used the auditorium.

The rock group, the American Breed, was to perform with a few other groups in a school promotion. The night of the concert, a winter blizzard hit and the American Breed barely made it to the show. The blizzard was so bad that the school considered calling off the concert but finally let it take place anyway.

Despite the blizzard, over 3,000 students jammed the concert hall and thousands were left outside to return home disappointed. The concert was a huge success.

Now I knew the American Breed very well. I knew the rock concert business, I knew the promotion business, and I knew how to advertise these shows.

So I decided to set up my own American Breed command performance in Traverse City to take place in May when the weather would be more predictable.

I planned two shows. My idea was to spend about $6,000 promoting the show to fill up the first performance and really do well on the second show.

I made professional radio announcements using professional announcers and I printed beautiful posters. I hired a few students at the college to promote the show, hang up the posters, and publicize the event.

I handled the show so professionally, and the American Breed was such a popular group in Traverse City, that I was convinced we would have a huge success.

The radio spots, the publicity, the posters, and all our promotion came off without a flaw. And on the day of the concert the weather was perfect. Instead of 3,000 for the first concert, we got 150, and the second concert drew 175. I lost my shirt.

I mentioned the above example as an illustration of timing and copying. Obviously something was wrong. I could give you dozens of reasons why I failed, but the overriding single most important reason was because I was copying a previous success.

Each problem or each situation has its own set of circumstances that are unique to it. Trying to copy another success does not force you to look at those unique circumstances that may demand an entirely different approach.

There is nothing wrong with innovation tempered with a little copying. Take for example what Mark O. Haroldson did. Haroldson read a book written by Joe Karbo entitled *A Lazy Man's Way to Riches*. The book explained how to use mail order to acquire wealth.

Haroldson then wrote his own ad fashioned after Joe Karbo's ad using suggestions from Karbo's book. But Haroldson offered his own concept, which was a blueprint for growing wealthy from real estate.

His first ads describing his "wealth formula" drew terrific response and he launched a very successful mail order book campaign that earned him millions of dollars.

Haroldson was a good example of building on the success of someone else but adding a personal touch of innovation.

I'm sure there are stories that tell how somebody copied something and succeeded. And I'm sure there are cases where someone copied somebody else and the timing was in fact better than the innovator, making the copycat more successful than the innovator. But these stories are rare.

If you've ever followed the record industry, you see many perfect examples of copying. When the Beatles became popular, there were hundreds of rock groups trying to imitate them. Nobody succeeded like they did. And instead of copying themselves, the Beatles constantly innovated, producing some of the most original music of their time.

We've all heard of rock singers who had one smash hit, then followed it up with what sounded like a copy of the first hit. The second record never sells as well as the first.

When I see somebody copying me, I am never worried. I would be concerned if I saw somebody innovating and selling the same products I do. Then I'd have some real competition.

So far I have not seen any innovators. Since most of my copiers feel that copying is the path to success, I have little to worry about.

Frank Schultz sells grapefruit through the mail. He had been selling grapefruit using direct mail, but whenever he went to an advertising agency to produce an advertisement he could run in a magazine or newspaper, the ad they produced did not succeed.

Schultz attended my mail order seminar and wrote an ad. The ad was a huge success and Schultz will probably be selling grapefruit for many years from that same advertisement. What he did was to take the same principles I use, but he innovated and produced what I consider one of the best mail order ads I've ever seen.

Copying seems like an easy way out, and I know that there are mail order books that preach copying as a way to success. But the only one making any money from those books is the author.

His approach to success might be innovative, so the author is doing well, but his advice isn't very good.

You might wonder how you can innovate. For starters, just avoid copying. Then realize that an innovator is someone who does things others think can't be done or who does things few people have done before.

Unfortunately, there is no exact formula for innovation. And since everything might appear to have already been invented, innovation might just be putting together the same things in a unique way.

The important point is that copying will bring you failure while innovation or doing it differently is a most powerful Success Force.

Clean Your Desk

One of the interesting things I've noted about successful people is how clean their desks are.

During my summer vacation breaks from college, one of my assignments while working for my father was to interview successful business executives who owned some of my father's printing equipment.

I was in charge of publishing a newspaper my father wanted to mail to his potential customers. It contained editorial material in addition to the usual hard-sell advertisements.

I felt that the readers of this paper would enjoy reading about successful printers who had purchased my father's equipment. I conducted at least ten interviews and observed a few things that seemed to be true about each company president.

At one point in their careers, each president had been told that his idea could not be done. And these presidents, convinced in their own minds that it could be done, took on the challenge to prove they were right. I have since learned that when somebody tells me that something can't be done, it should be a signal that there is a great opportunity if I can just prove that I'm right.

The second thing that all these people had in common was a clean desk. I wondered if these presidents did any work. And when I walked through their factories or printing plants, I was amazed at how clean and organized each of their facilities were.

Floors were clean, presses were polished, and files were neat. These companies gave you the feeling that they were very well managed and very efficient operations.

I always remembered my impressions from these interviews, and throughout my life I have always been aware of the role cleanliness played in a company's operation.

It was only when my company grew from a basement operation to a full-scale business in 1974 that I instituted many of my concepts on cleanliness and discipline.

We had grown so rapidly during 1974 that I had to resort to short cuts to keep the operation going smoothly, so the cleanliness and discipline I had believed in was postponed until we moved into our new deluxe office facility in Northbrook.

Our office facility was a single-story 6,000-square-foot office building—a far cry from our previous 1,000-square-foot office. All fifteen of our group fitted nicely into a portion of the space, and we purchased some new desks and chairs.

The building was built by a group of architects to reflect their creative ability. It was a spacious, high-quality building with eight-foot doors, a beautiful studio for me, beautiful lighting, and first-class treatment throughout. The impression you got from entering the building was unlike the one we projected in my basement or the corner store we had previously rented. We now projected the image that we were going to be around for a while and that we were a quality company.

But to carry that image forward we needed a clean-looking operation. Although we had more room and new desks, we still looked messy. At night papers were left in piles on the desks. There were labels, empty boxes, calculators—a variety of clutter that didn't fit the clean image of the building.

I remembered my previous newspaper interviews and subsequent observations and decided to implement a clean desk policy.

I insisted that all my employees clear off their desks before they left for home at night, and that nothing be left on their desks. This meant that even their "in" and "out" boxes had to be put away.

You can't imagine the complaints and moans I heard from my fifteen employees. But the main complaint was absolutely valid. They had no place to store all their papers.

I agreed with them and suspended the regulation until we could purchase additional file cabinets and desks to accommodate our work load.

When we received the desks and files, I once again announced my new clean desk policy. And once again my fifteen employees complained. Although we now had a place to put everything, we had no system of knowing what we had stored away. It was possible for a file to be stored and forgotten—one that required immediate action. Again my employees were correct. We indeed did not have the systems in place to handle the retrieval of files, and we had no auditing procedures to ensure that everything was indeed followed up.

Mary Stanke and I worked out procedures to ensure that everything that was put away at night could efficiently be brought out during the day.

Again, we instituted the clean desk policy and, surprisingly, with very few complaints. The employees now saw a much more efficient operation and felt considerably more at ease with the procedures.

Every night each desk was cleared and everything efficiently put away. If you walked into our offices at night, you'd think our Customer Service Department was an office furniture showroom. The floors were polished, the desks were clean, and everything was dusted and ready for the next big day.

There was no question in my mind of the efficiency of the operation. At the time, we had to handle hundreds of thousands of orders, pieces of paper and correspondence—and we handled them well because of the systems we employed.

Was it the clean desk that did the trick? Was it the employees' feelings of organization that caused their efficiency to improve? The clean desks were really manifestations of discipline. They were the direct reflection of how efficiently our company was being run.

I'm sure many of you with dirty desks may have a few valid reasons for keeping a dirty desk. You might work better with a cluttered desk. But remember that I'm not proposing that you work with a clean desk, just that you clear your desk at the end of the day. I work best on a large cluttered desk. But, at the end of the day, I put everything away.

You might be the type of person who works from eight in the morning until midnight and feel my concept may not apply to you. You're probably working too hard or you're not making better use of your time. You've either got to delegate, or refine your entire operation. You've got too much on your plate.

In the past, the excuse I had been using for not clearing off my desk at the end of the day was that I was putting in enormous hours. I then realized, that to keep a clean desk I would have to reduce my time. I was forced to think of logical steps to reduce my work load. In short, a clean desk represented a goal for me. If my desk remained cluttered, it was a negative signal.

I realize that cleaning your desk at the end of the day might sound like wasted effort, but it does work. It creates a Success Force to flush out the inconsistencies in your business efficiency. It forces you to organize your work, to organize your work load, and to put things in a proper perspective.

And it works! Not just for me, but for many of the people who have heard my speeches. People understand and relate to many of my philosophies, but the one philosophy that draws the most attention is the one on clean desks. I get letters from people who tell me how much cleaning their desk literally changed their lives and brought them success.

It's a Success Force that people can employ immediately to test my concept. Honesty, concentration, failure, and innovation are conceptual in nature, but clearing your desk can be done right after you close this book.

You may not have a desk to clean. Then how clear are the counters in your kitchen at night, or your workbench in the basement, or your desk in the garage, or the top drawer in your bedroom dresser? They are all really reflections of the cleanliness and discipline you must have to be successful.

A desk is also a good early warning indicator. Let's say you do clean your desk and get things organized and you are quite pleased with your newfound organization. Then one day you leave your desk dirty and, before long, you leave it dirty again. This should be a signal that you're doing something wrong or that your sloppiness is a symptom of something else that may be bothering you. Fine. Start figuring out why.

It could be just laziness, but what is suddenly causing that laziness? Is it because you are reluctant to tackle a big job? Why are you reluctant? By getting to the root or nature of your problem, you can often solve it quickly and achieve success.

Every time you clean your desk at the end of the day, you create a Success Force. Every time you don't clean your desk, you create a failure force.

And if others around you get into the habit of cleaning their desks at the end of the day, you suddenly find yourself better able to judge a problem before the problem gets serious through this unique early warning system.

An army experience I once had explains this concept from a general's point of view. When I was in the intelligence branch of the army, I met a girl who was the secretary to my commanding officer. Andrea's father was a colonel in the army and held a general's position.

I dated Andrea quite often and on occasion I would go to her house to pick her up, only to end up waiting for a half hour while she finished getting ready. This gave me the opportunity to talk to her father, who would often be sitting in his study.

One day we were discussing general staff inspections in which a general drives into a camp and conducts an examination of the camp's facilities, cleanliness, and staff.

What puzzled me about these inspections was that each general seemed to have a favorite thing he'd inspect. One general would pay particular attention to toilets—each toilet facility had to be so sparkling that (if you'll excuse the expression) you could eat off the floors.

Another general might select beds as his favorite target. Each camp had to have beds made up so perfectly and tightly that you could bounce a quarter off the blankets.

This general's target was windows. The panes and the windows had to be clean and sparkling inside and out.

Interesting, however, was the fact that the generals let their particular targets be known well in advance of their visit. It seemed that everybody knew what to concentrate on to prepare for the general's visit.

What puzzled me about the inspections was why the generals would let everybody know in advance what to do to please them. If I were conducting an inspection, I wouldn't say a thing. So I asked the general why he let his main concern be known in advance so that everybody could neglect the other things and concentrate on that one area.

"Simple," he replied. "If the troops know I'm keen on windows and I walk in and find dirty windows, I know immediately something is wrong and I really start examining things closely. If the windows are clean and dust-free, I know things are for the most part in order. I can tell in a few minutes a great deal about the morale and efficiency of a base."

Using the general's example, imagine how the same principle can be used to judge your company's performance. If you let it be known that clean desks are your "point of inspection," then a dirty desk would signal problems.

As long as the desks at JS&A are cleared off at night, I know things are functioning smoothly. The minute I see things left on desks, I get nosy and start snooping around. With a little effort, I usually find that there is a problem, and once it's corrected, the desks get cleaner.

If you have the will power to clean your desk at the end of the day, to organize your work properly and to put the work in a suitable container or file, you'll be well on the way to using one of my most effective Success Forces.

A clean desk, more than any other force, is easy to implement. Try it and see if it doesn't produce a very positive Success Force that you can usually measure within the first few months.

SECTION III

1
Success Philosophies

I have many success philosophies that go beyond the Success Force theory I've just presented.

I don't consider them in the same category as a Success Force. They do not have the same degree of effect on success that my Success Forces do. However, if you'll remember and follow them, they will be helpful in guiding you toward success.

In this section of the book, I will take my success philosophies and explain them, using some examples from my personal experiences.

Some of these philosophies you may have heard elsewhere, but in those cases my interpretation of them may be different. Others may be uniquely mine—except that I'm always amazed when I read of someone who lived ten centuries ago quoting my philosophy.

If you combine my success philosophies with my Success Forces, you can't help but be more successful.

Read this section carefully and study the examples. Refer to this section often. It will be a great help to you throughout your life.

2
Don't Let Ego Distort Good Business Sense

It's pretty hard to admit a mistake or a failure. We all have egos and whether they are big or small it still hurts our egos when we fail.

Your ego is one of your most important assets. It's a motivator that drives you on to bigger and better things. It keeps you going when times get rough.

But the dangerous part about ego is knowing when to put ego aside and accept failure, or when not to listen to your ego when you have to make an important decision.

Whenever I have let ego distort good business sense, I have suffered as a result. Whenever I was able to control my ego, I succeeded. It's just that simple.

I have seen large corporations refuse to abandon a product line even though they were losing a fortune, just for the sake of protecting their egos. Millions of dollars later, they finally

146

decided to drop the line quietly, but it was really too late. They had lost their shirts.

Another example is a reaction to somebody competing unfairly with you. I have seen a company run an advertisement opposite me and offer the same product at a lower price. My ego was hurt and I wanted revenge. But it was really only my ego that was upset. Good business sense dictated that I continue the course of action that made good business sense instead of one designed to get revenge and satisfy my wounded ego.

Revenge is a good example of letting your ego distort good business sense. Revenge is destructive. Taking a solid, mature course of action is the best way to go.

Another example of ego is when I complete what I think is a terrific ad only to test it and find out that the product doesn't sell. I'm sometimes tempted to keep running the ad even though I know I shouldn't.

I see that often with inventors. They're so proud of their invention that they get personally involved with it and refuse to let common sense guide them.

Whenever an ad doesn't work, a product doesn't sell, or a product cycle has ended, I drop it. There is no room for ego to distort good business sense.

Using ego for positive advantage is, however, a very powerful force. It gave me the guts to announce a five-day $2,000 marketing seminar at my estate in northern Wisconsin that was quickly sold out. It drives me to create the very best mail order advertising I can produce.

Your ego is powerful. Used in a positive way with common sense, it works and it works wonders. Letting it distort good business sense can cost you a fortune and increase your chances of failure. Get to know your ego. And make it your best friend.

3
Become an Expert

No concept is more powerful than becoming an expert in whatever you endeavor to undertake.

If you own a store that sells leather goods, then become an expert on leather. Visit a tannery. See how leather is processed. Study the history of leather and how it evolved. Keep up to date on the latest leather technology and monitor your competition.

Having a thorough knowledge of a particular subject will open more doors for you and bring you greater success than you'll ever believe.

Becoming an expert has its limitations, too. I contend that you should become an expert to the extent necessary to fulfull your perception or goal.

If your plans are to sell leather, it might be a waste of your time to actually tan leather or learn how cattle are slaughtered before the hides are removed. There's a practical limit to how much you need to know.

I have sat in on seminars conducted at direct marketing conventions and cringed as the so-called experts told their audiences they *shouldn't* become experts. In the entire history of running my company and writing hundreds of advertisements, every one of my most successful ads resulted from my becoming an expert on the product—to a limit—and then writing the advertisement. I can cite two beautiful examples of this concept.

I was approached at the Consumer Electronics Show in June of 1975 and presented with a new product about to be manufactured in Hong Kong.

The product was presented to me as a miniature walkie-talkie. It measured only ½ inch by 1½ inches by 5 inches, and it fit into a pocket, so it was a handy device, but I needed more information so I could explain why the unit was so small, how it operated, and what would appeal to the consumer.

I met with the engineers and they explained how sensitive the unit's receiver was, how well the transmitter performed, and how the integrated circuits functioned in the unit.

But something was missing. I still hadn't found the really exciting way to present the product until the engineers started to talk about the transmitter frequency. The engineer mentioned that it transmitted on the 27 megahertz frequency. I delved further.

"What other products broadcast on that frequency?" I questioned.

The engineers told me that the CB bands used the frequency and 27 megahertz was in fact CB channel 14.

That was the grabber I was looking for. The CB craze was just beginning and the fact that the miniature walkie-talkie broadcast on channel 14 gave me my headline—"Pocket CB."

The sales soared. Unfortunately, the manufacturer had production delays, but when we finally delivered, the pocket CB turned out to be one of the most successful products in our history.

Another example of becoming an expert (to a certain extent) was for a new digital watch we were about to announce.

The manufacturer, Micro Display Systems in Dallas, Texas, had given us their first watch to introduce one year earlier. The watch represented a breakthrough in digital watch design because it incorporated a liquid crystal display and a small night light. During the day you could read the digital display without pressing a button and at night you pressed the night light to illuminate the display.

The new watch represented a major advance over even the previous model. It had a light that glowed automatically in the dark so there was no button to press at all—day or night. But how was I to convey this fact?

I started to become an expert. I talked to the engineers at length. Then I came upon an interesting fact when discussing the glow-in-the-dark light source.

It seemed that the light source used a material called tritium that, when combined with phosphor and instantly sealed, created a phosphorescent glow. I investigated further.

I then asked for a description of how the capsule was sealed, only to discover that a laser beam was used. In fact, the whole process was impossible to perform until the laser beam process was developed for sealing the tritium/phosphor capsule.

That's all I needed to know. I used the headline "Laser Beam Digital Watch" and proceeded to explain how the new watch breakthrough was made possible by the use of a laser beam.

The watch sold quite well. In both of the examples above I strove to become an expert. When I had just enough facts, the marketing solutions popped out.

Becoming an expert is a sure way to grow. I can remember an employee of ours who often complained that he had a lot of untapped potential that was going to waste. He wanted to get into some responsible sales position to sell our pocket CB unit, but, he said, he wasn't given the chance. But for someone who wanted to get into CB sales, he knew nothing about CB. If I had been him, I would have become an expert on sales and CB, devoured all the books on the subjects, and then approached us. Even after he did talk to us, and I suggested that he should first become an expert on the subjects of CB and sales, he never did.

Joe Girard, the super-successful car salesman in Detroit, is no expert on cars. He found early in the game that he didn't have to be. He did, however, become an expert on motivation, service, and sales techniques, and he uses these skills with great success.

If I were going to be an insurance salesman, I'd learn everything I could about sales, insurance, and people. The best sales reps that sell us products are those who not only are experts on their products but also know a great deal about JS&A.

The more you become an expert on a subject, the more information you have in your mental data bank and the more information you'll be able to recall when you need it.

I'd like to relate a true story about something that happened to me in high school that best explains why it pays to become an expert.

I was a junior at the time and a beautiful blond girl (in those days a blond was naturally blond) from California started attending our high school.

Betty Jane was so beautiful that even those handsome senior football players were too awestruck even to walk up to her and start a conversation. To watch her walk down the hall was an experience in itself. All heads would turn and everybody would stare. The poor girl was having a rough time blending in—that's for sure.

I had a brainstorm. If I really wanted to get to know Betty Jane, what could I do? I had heard that she was from San Diego and used that as the premise of my new plan. I had deduced that anybody from San Diego living in the Chicago area would have to be homesick. What if somebody approached her who was also from San Diego? She would have something to talk about and would probably enjoy sharing her experiences and memories. So I proceeded to be that somebody.

I went to my local library and got all the books I could on San Diego. I wrote the San Diego Chamber of Commerce, the San Diego Port Authority, the San Diego Zoo, the San Diego Board of Education, and the San Diego Road Commission.

I then read everything I could on the city, its people, the schools, its recreation. I even made a few long-distance calls, interviewed some people from San Diego, and after almost two months I became an expert on San Diego. I knew enough to discuss the schools, where the kids hung out, the latest fads, the places to go, the most popular drive-ins and movie houses, and even some of the slang. I was an expert in the true tradition of my concept.

And I also studied Betty Jane's movements. I knew that on Tuesdays and Thursdays at 9 A.M. she had a class near my locker, and that at 9:03 A.M. she would walk by my locker, usually alone, and pass within three feet of me.

So I planned to wait until she was a few feet away, whirl, and then start talking to her. I was not only prepared on San Diego, but I also had my timing down to a science.

I'll never forget that day. I dressed in my very best high school clothes. I had a clean slick haircut, had scrubbed my face and was prepared for my pitch. I was ready.

It was a Thursday, and from the corner of my eye I saw Betty Jane walking out of her classroom. I held some books in my hand, shut my locker door just as she was approaching. Then I turned, "Betty Jane, I understand you're from San Diego?"

Betty Jane turned, smiled, and said, "No, I'm from Sacramento."

I don't remember what happened after that—whether I fainted, bumbled, collapsed, or whatever. It's a memory that somehow fades after the word "Sacramento," but it does illustrate my concept: become an expert—but don't believe everything you hear.

4
Don't Give Up

One of the overriding reasons for my success is that I never gave up until I had no choice. Call it persistence, ego—but I never felt right unless I had given it everything I had. I was a fighter—not with fists and gloves, but with ideas, effort, and persistence. If I felt I had an idea that was good, I took it to its logical conclusion. I never gave up until the handwriting was on the wall.

Through all my failures, I always held the philosophy that even if I lost, it was an experience I could put in my back pocket and some day reach in and pull it out.

The real world is full of traps, failures, and disappointments. I often wonder if they're there to test us as we strive for success. If you can withstand these pitfalls and not give up, success often follows.

There's a thin line between my philosophies of "never give up" and "don't let ego distort good business sense." I'll leave it to you to decide where that line is. The best way to determine this would be to ask yourself a question: "Do I feel there's still a chance for success and is it worth the effort?" If the answer is "yes," then don't give up. If the answer is "no," you're probably trying to satisfy your ego.

Never give up. It's pretty important advice.

5
The Truth Always Emerges

I once gave a speech in Mexico City at the Direct Mail Marketing Association annual convention. One of the keynote speakers at the convention was Ben Bradlee, Editor-in-Chief of the *Washington Post*. Bradlee gave the audience a little insight into the Watergate scandal and told how his people blew the whistle and exposed the whole thing.

But what I got out of his speech was something I've observed in my lifetime but was never able to put into words—namely, if you wait long enough, the truth will emerge.

Think about it. A weekly magazine report on an incident is often more accurate and truthful than a newspaper story on the same event. The newspaper can't afford to wait, so it publishes what it has as quickly as it can. It doesn't have the perspective of a weekly magazine that can take all the newspaper reports and paint a more accurate picture.

And take a report from a monthly magazine doing a story

previously covered by a weekly news magazine. Very often it is far more accurate than the weekly magazine's report, which was put together with all the data it could gather during that week.

The history books offer yet another version of the event. Presidents are often judged thirty or forty years after they die. Facts about Kennedy's romances while president are just now surfacing.

And so it is in your life. I have found that when an important decision has to be made, waiting a little longer sometimes helps in gathering more facts to reach the truth.

If somebody lies to me and I am unaware of it at the time, I eventually find out. The truth always emerges. All you have to do is have the patience to wait.

Please don't use this philosophy as an excuse to procrastinate. But when you are unsure of yourself, waiting sometimes flushes out all the facts you need to make a really good decision.

Remember this philosophy. See how it has worked in history. See how it works in your daily life. Once you understand and appreciate this philosophy, you'll be amazed at how much better your decisions become.

The truth always emerges.

6
Life Is a Moving Target

We have an electronic game in our basement at our estate in northern Wisconsin called "Sea Wolf." It consists of various boats going across a TV screen at different speeds. You use a periscope with cross hairs to aim at the boats and you press a button to release a torpedo that moves slowly through the waves before it strikes the target. Every time you strike a boat with a torpedo you score some points.

The faster a boat moves across the screen, the more points you get, but in order to hit it you've got to fire your torpedo well enough ahead of its projected course. A PT boat worth 700 points zips across the screen so fast that you have to fire within seconds of its appearance and well in advance of its projected course. A slow-moving freighter is worth only 100 points, but you have plenty of time to hit it almost dead on.

The game repeats the same cycle every nine boats. Once you

realize this and can remember this cycle you can improve your accuracy by anticipating the next boat.

The game, in my opinion, is a good analogy of life. In fact, at my seminars I urge my students to play the game throughout my course. At the end of the course we discuss its significance and how life parallels this unique game.

First of all, life is a moving target. The Chinese say that the only thing constant in life is change.

If you'll view life as a series of moving targets, you will find that some targets move fast, requiring you to lead the target before you fire, and others require you to shoot straight ahead. For those fast-moving, hard-to-shoot targets you score more points, so to be very successful in life you've got to be prepared to try tougher challenges.

Life is really a series of targets. But in life they may not look like targets, nor do you shoot at them.

To score in life you first have to realize that everything does move and change relationships. Knowing this you can expect change and be better able to accept it.

The person whom you married more than likely has changed— hopefully enough to complement your changes. Expecting this change can help you accept your partner.

Your business changes. Competition, technology, the economy, and consumer moods are changing all the time. Awareness of these changes and their direction will help you take aim.

"The world is a moving target and a computer helps you to take aim," was IBM's appropriate slogan to sell their computers. A computer condenses the time and the information you need to point your company in the proper direction. And pointed in the proper direction with the proper timing, your shots can score points you wouldn't previously score.

There is no great step-by-step procedure I can leave with you for improving your aim or to help you score more points. But you should be aware that change is a fact of life, and that life is a moving target. The faster the target, the more points you score if your aim is right.

7
Humility

One of the amazing things I discovered about success was that those people who are truly successful and have reached a high level of self-actualization are very humble people. The people who are failures are the most arrogant.

At JS&A we have even discovered a little test that helps me separate the successful people from the failures. When people call me at my office, I am often busy in meetings or working in my studio, and I have my secretary take messages for me. I've asked her to take as much information about the call as possible so I can at least determine the priority of my calls when I have time to call back.

Whenever somebody calls and is arrogant, disrespectful, and discourteous to my secretary in an effort to get through to me, these people usually turn out to be failures in life. The contrast between the way they talk to me and the way they talk to her is incredible. I have often overheard some of these conversations that sound as they come from two entirely separate people.

On the other hand, my secretary didn't know the name Charles Tandy, so when the late chairman of the board of the very successful Tandy Corporation, the parent company of Radio Shack, stopped through Chicago and wanted to see me, he was understanding and pleasant and calmly left his message.

As soon as I recognized the correlation between humility, failure, and success, I started observing those who had been disrespectful to my secretary. I made it an effort to get to know them a little better. I also met with a number of people who were very courteous to my secretary.

From these observations I discovered that the truly successful people in life were genuinely humble. The truly arrogant and disrespectful individuals were often people who were failures. Their lack of humility may have indeed played an important role in their failure.

I also found a Chinese saying that says with humility you will never have to worry about failure.

All my life I have repeated time and again one philosophy about success—namely, that if I am fortunate enough to be successful, I will remain humble. For any truly successful person will tell you that it is only when you are indeed successful that you realize how important every person is regardless of his or her station in life.

8
Cycles

I have built my success on a philosophy of cycle watching. I realized early that practically everything in life is cyclical. The stock market, consumer moods, economics, nature—everything rises and falls, usually in a regular rhythm.

I first became aware of this phenomenon when I took advanced physics in college. It was a very rough course but one of my most interesting. For the first time since I started school, all my previous math courses made sense. I was using advanced calculus, geometry, statistics, and dynamics, and they were fitting together as useful tools to solve very complex physics problems.

But I also learned that in many a physics equation—whether it involved fluids, solids, gases, or whether it was discovered by a physicist 200 years ago or just recently—there was always the constant pi in the equation, or 3.1416. This number, when multiplied by the diameter of a circle, gave you the circumference of that circle.

A circle is in essence a cycle—one complete revolution. It led me to believe that all of nature is cyclical or has its peaks and valleys. But then I started studying other forms of nature.

I learned that many things have cycles in almost an uncanny and predictable way; for example, the eleven-year peak in salmon production, and the seventeen-year locusts. Even the stock market and the economy have their cycles.

In my years at JS&A I built my business on being able to sense the start of a cycle, follow it to its practical peak and get out in time to go on to another emerging cycle. I never tried to follow the cycle beyond its peak.

Every event in life is a combination of many cycles. Take my business, for example. During one year, more expensive items will sell best; during the next year, inexpensive items. There may be a lull in consumer confidence, but one product may be selling better than another. And the list goes on.

It was up to me to sense these cycles and somehow develop strategies to concentrate on the upward movements and to avoid those cycles that would be declining.

It is my opinion that thousands of cycles affect our lives every day. Being able to sense or detect these cycles is one of the keys to success. Many successful businessmen can "feel" or have a "gut feel" for a situation. Some call it intuition.

Feeling the cycle is very often based on experience. And having enough experience, enough failures, and enough facts will give you that feel.

We tend to avoid situations in life that are unpleasant to us and feel attracted to situations that make us feel good. It's the same principle with cycles. We are going to be attracted to making moves based on feeling good about the facts we know and the feelings we have about a situation.

Let me cite two examples of products that ran their cycles, peaked, and then flattened.

The printing calculator was a sensation in 1974 when prices dropped to around $100 and the market really opened up. Casio, a Japanese company, had presented me with a printing calculator it was planning to sell for $150.

I thought the item was good. It had an unusual printing head, had good quality and the unit looked good. But Casio saw that they weren't selling too well so they dropped their price to $100 retail at a cost to me of $70. The ad I ran for the unit was a huge success, tempered only by the fact that Casio couldn't supply us with enough of them.

In 1978, four years later, Canon approached us with a printing calculator. The printing calculator market was poor. I felt that the market looked as if a printing calculator might just make a comeback and be successful again. We tried a test and our hunch was correct. We sold 20,000 Canon printing calculators and revived the cycle in the United States for all dealers. We'll try a printing calculator again in 1982 when the cycle once more starts to rise.

The telephone answering unit is another example of starting a cycle. These units were once popular, but sales had recently been flat. I had a gut feel that there could be an upswing in the market for this type of unit, so I selected the Ford Code-A-Phone, which I thought was the best unit on the market at the time, and ran it in an advertising campaign. We sold thousands of them for three solid years.

We've been responsible for starting cycles for calculators, pinball games, security systems, micro recorders, telephones, and a multitude of other products—which may explain why the retailing giants like Sears, Ward, Penney, and all the discount chains watch us carefully.

I'm writing this chapter in Maui, an island in the Hawaiian Island chain. I came here to write a portion of this book but also to buy a condominium as an investment. I couldn't believe the prices here—$250,000 for a one-bedroom unit that would sell for $60,000 on the mainland. I'm too late. If I was thinking of getting in on this cycle, I was near its peak—but certainly not at its beginning. Prices have been going up at a rate of 45 percent a year, and at that rate I definitely missed the start of the cycle.

In fact, as a general rule, when you hear of a tremendous opportunity in which others have made a lot of money, it's often too late. The cycle is probably near its peak or on the way down.

Always look for the ground floor opportunity and ride the cycle up. It is the riskiest time, and when you look at the opportunity it will have the appearance of a deal that could go sour. But that's how I've discovered my greatest growth opportunities.

In the stock market, going against the general direction of the crowd usually brings the greatest success. When the herd is stampeding in one direction, the astute stock owner is sensing the start of the next trend and preparing for it.

The start of a cycle is never obvious. It is only after you have discovered you were right that it becomes obvious. But recognizing the start of a cycle upswing in anything you do will add great benefits to your potential success.

There are cycles in your personal life, too. A friend of mine, Bernard Gittelson, wrote a book entitled *Biorhythm—A Personal Science*, in which he explains that our bodies have regular cycles, too. Some days we're up; other days we're down.

You may not subscribe to his theory, but it is a good study of how a series of cycles can affect your moods and your physical and mental abilities.

The Chinese have an entire philosophy about cycles. Called I Ching, the concept is based on our brains being subconsciously programmed to sense cycles.

I wrote an advertisement on I Ching for a product we sold, but the copy is so appropriate for this chapter that I would like to reproduce it here.

CRYSTAL BALL TECHNOLOGY
A Game, a gimmick, or a major breakthrough in predicting the future? You be the judge.

As incredible as this may sound, there may be a way to predict the future. But because of the very sensitive implications, we will leave all conclusions to the reader.

American scientists have developed a computer that, together with the science of cycles, an ancient Chinese theory, and the electrical impulses and sensing mechanism of the human brain, permits you to read your subconscious mind.

The small computer has only two buttons and three lights. But before we describe its uses, you must first understand three basic concepts.

CONCEPT 1: THE SCIENCE OF CYCLES

Any student of economics, natural science, or the stock market knows that events happen in cycles. Sunspots, weather conditions, the economy, birth rates, wholesale prices, crime, and wars—all follow a pattern or cycle.

CONCEPT 2: THE HUMAN BRAIN

The human brain processes data through electrical impulses. This concept was defined by Dr. Norbert Wiener in his 1948 book entitled *Cybernetics*. He stated that the brain handles the electrical impulses using the binary code—the same code used by computers. This theory has since been endorsed by many scientists.

CONCEPT 3: THE CHINESE THEORY

Over 3,000 years ago, the Chinese developed a system of predicting the future through a series of mathematical formulas based on the theory of probability and a series of biological relationships between objects. Called "I Ching," it was more a system of predicting the probability of success than actually predicting the future. In order to understand this system, you must understand three aspects of the I Ching concept: (1) It uses binary code discovered by the Chinese over 3,000·years ago; (2) It is based on the scientific theories of probability; and (3) It is based on relationships commonly found in dreams.

THE DREAM RELATIONSHIPS

When you drop a stone in a pond of water, you create a ripple effect in the water at a specific frequency. If you drop an apple, an orange, or an old shoe and by coincidence create the same frequency, you have a relationship between all of these objects even though none of them seems related. The Chinese theory states that there are just such biological relationships in life.

Recent psychological studies of dreams have confirmed this.

For example, the theory of I Ching says that a relationship exists between a lake, autumn, wood, the youngest daughter, the mouth, and the wind. The Chinese theory further states that all these things have a common frequency or vibration similar to the hypothetical example of the pebble, apple, orange, and the old shoe.

In tests performed by leading psychiatrists under controlled conditions, these related objects appeared with startling frequency in the dreams of subjects.

Carl Jung, one of the fathers of modern psychiatry, studied I Ching. Jung's theory and the theory of I Ching state that the various relationships proven to exist in dreams are subconsciously programmed in our brain. And like the pebble and water example, these relationships have their own rhythms and cycles.

YOUR BRAIN DETECTS CYCLES

Our brain cells, according to the theory, detect and register their cycles. The brain then compares our own cycles with those of hundreds of outside cycles at a given time. In the comparison process, our body and mind are subconsciously directed toward conditions helpful to our development and avoid those which are not. The best example of this theory is the survival reaction of animals who can detect an earthquake days before the actual event, something man cannot do with the most sophisticated measuring instruments.

PUTTING IT ALL TOGETHER

The degree to which we are compatible with another person or situation is therefore how our specific set of biological relationships and cycles at a specific moment are in phase with another event, situation, or person.

If we are in phase, the theory states, we will achieve success without much effort. If we are out of phase, the theory states that our chances of failure are greater. It does not determine our fate but rather tells us the probability of compatibility with that person or situation at a specific time. If we are told that our compatibility with a situation will be out of phase, we still have an opportunity to work against or adjust to that probability and still achieve success.

THE I CHING SYSTEM

The ancient I Ching system is described in terms of a game in the *Scientific American* cover story of January, 1974. The steps in the game were long and complicated but designed to transfer the subconscious expressions of compatibility to the real and visual symbols needed to interpret these expressions. Sixty-four sticks were used along with enough movement and decisions to let a person's subconscious express itself through physical motions and a binary application to the theory of probability.

So accurate were the results of this process that emperors used it to rule their countries. 250 books were written on its effectiveness and many leading scientists feel that the I Ching concept was taught to the Chinese from a distant civilization—that no group of scholars 3,000 years ago could have invented it.

There was one drawback to the I Ching system. After you determined the exact combination of sticks, you then had to look in a book of 64 formulas and interpret the relationships and their compatibilities to your specific situation. This required the great scholars of China who understood these relationships and the binary code. There are very few people who can do all this today.

Recently a group of American scientists took the 64 basic formula relationships expressed in binary code and devised a computer that selects the correct formula and translates the results.

WHAT COULD THE I CHING COMPUTER DO FOR YOU?

The great leaders of history were superior people who let intuition guide them and took decisive action, often in the face of unsurmountable odds. We all have the same opportunity of being a superior person by letting ourselves recognize our intuitive or "gut" feelings and then taking action.

Often, just taking action achieves success. All too frequently, people go through life saying, "Had I only done something."

Indecision is to failure as decision is to success.

The I Ching concept puts us in touch with another dimension of ourselves—that of the superior person inside all of us. It permits us to let intuition or "gut" feelings play a more important role in our decision-making process, and finally, it puts us in touch with ourselves by letting us tune into ourselves.

You make most of your decisions based on available data. With little data, you make decisions based on intuition, so in these situations, the I Ching computer can be like a wise friend.

EASY TO USE

To use the computer, you just press the left button with your thumb. This starts a sequential generator similar to a roulette wheel which scans the 64 basic I Ching formulas.

You concentrate deeply on a goal or question: "Should I invest in the stock market?" "Should I accept the date?" Then you press the button on the right at the exact moment your subconscious tells you to. Each one of the 64 formulas rotates in exactly three milliseconds (three one-thousandths of a second), the exact time required for a human to respond to a signal from the brain through the nervous system.

The computer is a small ($1\frac{1}{2}'' \times 2\frac{1}{2}'' \times 3\frac{1}{2}''$), yet very sophisticated system using a double ion implant P-Channel MOS integrated microprocessor-type circuit. It generates and stops at a specific formula and interprets this formula through the binary code and a series of three lights—each with three different color combinations which are then easy to interpret.

You can use it as a helpful decision maker, as a party conversation piece, or as a unique gift. We do not wish to make claims as to its effectiveness, but the fact that our company is offering this product is the strongest statement we can make about the computer and the validity of the concept. The system's accuracy will either send chills up your spine or end up as just another conversation piece. Could it be hundreds of years ahead of its time, or is its timing perfect? You can decide.

To order your I Ching Computer, send your check for $29.95 plus $2.50 for postage and handling. By return mail, you will receive your unit with complete instructions for interpreting the results and a one-year limited warranty. You also have a 30-day trial period. If you are not pleased with your unit, return it for a full refund including your $2.50 postage.

Space-age scientists may have just discovered a way to read your subconscious and determine your probabilities of success through the use of a computer. Order your I Ching Computer and find out at no obligation today.

9
Strive for Excellence

In examining the lives of really successful people I have discovered another trait that seems to characterize their lives.

These people, when faced with accepting mediocre work, rejected it and spent the money and risked the time to produce the best possible results.

When Joe Siegel, formerly of the Franklin Mint, ran the company, if everything wasn't perfect, he'd redo it, often throwing away thousands of dollars of printing during a time when the mint couldn't afford it.

When I produce an advertisement for my company and see a word or phrase that would improve the ad, I stop the presses or hold up a publication while I make the correction. I'm certainly not perfect, and many mistakes have slipped through my hands, but I strive for excellence.

I'm not a perfectionist. A perfectionist is a portrait in frustration. Rarely, if ever, is perfection achieved. But excellence is something else. My advertising is excellent. Not perfect. And in order to make it excellent, I really have to work at it.

No matter what you do, strive for excellence. Don't accept sloppy work. Remember that everything you do is a direct reflection on you and you should look good at anything worth doing.

You are often going to be confronted with a choice while striving for excellence. If you remember that every time you opt for excellent over average, you're tipping the scale toward greater success.

10
The 80/20/30 Rule

You've all heard of the 80/20 rule in its many forms. It is said, for example, that 20 percent of a company's employees usually produce 80 percent of the work. Or that 20 percent of your time is productive and you waste the other 80 percent.

My philosophy goes beyond the standard concept of the 80/20 rule in that it suggests an action that will result in 30 percent more profit; hence the 80/20/30 rule.

I say that in business 20 percent of your profits create 80 percent of your headaches. For example, you might have ten clients, eight of which are just great but two of which create 80 percent of your problems. They pay late, fail to live up to their promises, and cause you a great deal of unproductive work.

My rule says that if you sacrifice the 20 percent of your profits that creates 80 percent of your headaches, you'll end up making 30 percent more profit.

Think about it. Eliminate those two headache accounts, or 20 percent of your profits—and what happens? First, you'll have more time to devote to your really good accounts. Your time will be more productive and you'll be able to make room for another good account. You'll soon find that by getting rid of your headaches, even though they represent 20 percent of your profits, you'll end up with a 30 percent higher profit and greater peace of mind.

This rule can be applied to many situations. For example, at one point in JS&A's history, we accepted purchase orders from major corporations for the purchase of calculators. This activity represented 20 percent of our volume.

However, the program required three people to follow up on the late payments and a great deal more paperwork. We found that many people who bought on credit tended to use our products, never pay for them, and return them months later.

One day I decided to eliminate open account billings and request checks from anyone purchasing our products. It represented 20 percent of our business and theoretically 20 percent of our profits, but it also represented 80 percent of our headaches.

It didn't take me more than a few months to realize that it was the best move I ever made. The three people I needed to collect on delinquent accounts were soon reassigned to other areas of the company, which gave us the opportunity to expand. There was less trouble with returned products, and we were saving a great deal of time and effort. Most of our credit customers started paying by check. Our business actually grew as a result of this move.

Take a look at the areas in your life that create 80 percent of your headaches. The best way to do that is to first select those areas that you really enjoy and those areas you do best in. Then make a list of those areas you do poorly in and don't enjoy.

You'll be amazed to discover that the unpleasant areas that cause you 80 percent of your aggravation and discomfort represent only 20 percent of your activities. Simply by eliminating those areas (often at what appears to be a sacrifice) your life will improve, you'll be happier and you'll profit overall from the move.

11
Success Pressures

We've already discussed Success Forces and how they work. Let us assume that you will use some of the Success Forces to force you to be more successful. Great. But be careful.

For success—all success—has its associated pressures. Again, it's a case of equal and opposite reaction. Once you've achieved success a pressure tends to develop to offset your success. So expect it and be sure you have examined the possible pressures to determine whether or not you're willing to make the sacrifice and commitment to be successful.

I own a Mercedes Benz 450 SLC. It cost me $38,000 when I bought it and, aside from its good ride and great resale value, the car is a beauty.

But with my super car, I have the associated pressures. I can't drive it everywhere for fear of theft. I'm reluctant to let any parking lot attendant park it. I avoid leaving it in parking lots

174

for fear of what other car doors will do to its exterior. And vandals choose cars like mine to scratch with their keys.

Maybe I'm overly protective of my car, but it's my style with things like that. I take great pride in the things I own and would not want them destroyed or stolen.

A while back I gave my 450 SLC to Mary Stanke, JS&A's executive vice president. To her it's a pressure she doesn't mind living with. I'm now driving a 1974 Oldsmobile Toronado. It's rusted in spots with a few nicks and dents, and two of the hub caps are missing. But I'm quite happy with it. I have none of the pressures I felt with my Mercedes.

I can drive the Oldsmobile anywhere, leave it with parking lot attendants, not worry about anybody stealing it, and not attract too much attention.

Mary loves the Mercedes. She's more than willing to accept the pressures because it's a status symbol—one that she never imagined she'd attain. To me the pressure was not worth the status.

Again, I use this example to indicate that indeed pressures are imposed once you achieve success, and these pressures may not be evident as you climb the ladder.

Let's take another example that has recently posed serious problems for families, causing many of them to break up.

It usually happens to a family in which one of the partners is overweight and goes on a weight reduction program. The heavy partner feels pressure once the weight is off. He or she becomes more attractive to the opposite sex. Inspired by this newfound attention, new relationships develop, and suddenly conflicts arise.

Psychologists have studied this phenomenon and have found that some people develop such strong pressures along with their new figures that they start eating again to escape.

Again, success has its associated pressures. And every success-ful achievement has been slightly offset by the achievement's negative pressures. We are not suggesting you avoid the chance of success, the opportunity to buy an exciting new car, or the desire to lose weight. Just be prepared to expect a pressure that takes a little of the luster of success away once you achieve it. Often the pressures cannot be predicted. How do you know what it's like to enjoy a great car when you've never owned one?

If you are aware of the success pressures and realize that they do develop, you'll be better prepared to cope with them when they happen.

At JS&A we too have felt the success pressures as a company. They've come from dishonest consumers who feel our success entitles them to take advantage of us. They've come from unethical competitors who unfairly and untruthfully attack our product offerings to further their sales at our expense. And they've come from government regulators whose envy of successful businesses often translates into vengeful acts that accomplish no useful purpose.

But that is the price our company has had to pay. Success indeed has its own associated pressures that often take the luster off the successful goal you've reached.

An excellent example of many of the principles in this book and especially of success pressures can be found in the next chapter on my battle with the Federal Trade Commission. JS&A had achieved an envied level of success and accomplishment. We were a very visible company that was looked up to as a leader not only in electronics but in marketing as well. We were ripe for the FTC.

SECTION IV

1
Success Forces
and My Battle with the FTC

On November 6, 1979, I ran a daring advertisement in the *Wall Street Journal*, the *Washington Post*, and the *New York Times* in response to my harassment at the hands of the Chicago office of the FTC. The FTC investigators were trying to extract a large and unfair penalty from our company. The ad read as follows:

FTC REVOLT
You've heard of the tax revolt. It's about time for an FTC revolt. Here's my story and why we've got to stop federal bureaucratic regulation.

BY JOSEPH SUGARMAN,
PRESIDENT JS&A GROUP, INC.

My story is only one example of how the FTC is harassing small businesses but I'm not going to sit back and take it.

I'm pretty lucky. When I started my business in my basement eight years ago, I had little more than an idea and a product.

The product was the pocket calculator. The idea was to sell it through advertisements in national magazines and newspapers.

Those first years in the basement weren't easy. But, we worked hard and through imaginative advertising and a dedicated staff, JS&A grew rapidly to become well recognized as an innovator in electronics and marketing.

THREE BLIZZARDS

In January of 1979, three major blizzards struck the Chicago area. The heaviest snowfall hit Northbrook, our village—just 20 miles north of Chicago.

Many of our employees were stranded—unable to get to our office where huge drifts made travel impossible. Not only were we unable to reach our office, but our computer totally broke down leaving us in even deeper trouble.

But we fought back. Our staff worked around the clock and on weekends. First, we processed orders manually. We also hired a group of computer specialists, rented outside computer time, employed a computer service bureau, and hired temporary help to feed this new computer network. We never gave up. Our totally dedicated staff and the patience of many of our customers helped us through the worst few months in our history. Although there were many customers who had to wait over 30 days for their parcels, every package was eventually shipped.

WE OPENED OUR DOORS

During this period, some of our customers called the FTC (Federal Trade Commission) to complain. We couldn't blame them. Despite our efforts to manually notify our customers of our delays, our computer was not functioning making the task extremely difficult.

The FTC advised JS&A of these complaints. To assure the FTC that we were a responsible company, we invited them to visit us. During their visit we showed them our computerized microfilm system which we use to back up every transaction. We showed them our new dual computer system (our main system and a backup system in case our main system ever failed again). And, we demonstrated how we were able to locate and trace every order. We were very cooperative, allowing them to look at every document they requested.

The FTC left. About one week later, they called and told us that they wanted us to pay a $100,000 penalty for not shipping our products within their 30-day rule. (The FTC rule states that anyone paying by check is entitled to have their purchase shipped within 30 days or they must be notified and given the option to cancel.)

NOT BY CONGRESS

The FTC rule is not a law nor a statute passed by Congress, but rather a rule created by the FTC to strengthen their enforcement powers. I always felt that the rule was intended to be used against companies that purposely took advantage of the consumer. Instead, it appears that the real violators, who often are too difficult to prosecute, get away while JS&A, a visible and highly respected company that pays taxes and has contributed to our free enterprise system, is singled out. I don't think that was the intent of the rule.

And when the FTC goes to court, they have the full resources of the U.S. government. Small, legitimate businesses haven't got a chance.

We're not perfect. We do make mistakes. But if we do make a mistake, we admit it, accept the responsibility, and then take whatever measures necessary to correct it. That's how we've built our reputation.

BLOW YOUR KNEE CAPS OFF

Our attorneys advised us to settle. As one attorney said, "It's like a bully pulling out a gun and saying, 'If you don't give me a nickel, I'll blow your knee caps off.'" They advised us that the government will subpoena thousands of documents to harass us and cause us great inconvenience. They warned us that even if we went to court and won, we would end up spending more in legal fees than if we settled.

To settle would mean to negotiate a fine and sign a consent decree. The FTC would then issue a press release publicizing their victory.

At first we tried to settle. We met with two young FTC attorneys and agreed in principle to pay consumers for any damages caused them. But there were practically no damages, just a temporary computer problem, some late shipments, and some bad weather. The FTC then issued a massive subpoena requesting documents that will take us months to gather and which we feel was designed to harass or force us to accept their original $100,000 settlement request.

Remember, the FTC publicizes their actions. And the higher the fine, the more the publicity and the more stature these two attorneys will have at the FTC.

If this all sounds like blackmail—that's just what it appeared to be to us.

We did ship our products late—something we've admitted to them and which we publicly admit here, but we refuse to be blackmailed into paying a huge fine at the expense of our company's reputation—something we've worked hard eight years to build.

We're not a big company and we realize it would be easier to settle now at any cost. But we're not. If this advertisement can attract the attention of congressmen and senators who have the power to stop the harassment of Americans by the FTC, then our efforts will be well spent.

ALL AMERICANS AFFECTED

Federal regulations and the whims of a few career-building bureaucrats are costing tax-payers millions, destroying our free enterprise system, affecting our productivity as a nation, and as a result is lowering everybody's standard of living.

I urge congressmen, senators, businessmen, and above all, the consumer to support legislation to take the powers of the FTC from the hands of a few unelected officials and bring them back to Congress and the people.

I will be running this advertisement in hundreds of magazines and newspapers during the coming months. I'm not asking for contributions to support my effort as this is my battle, but I do urge you to send this advertisement to your congressmen and senators. That's how you can help.

America was built on the free enterprise system. Today, the

FTC is undermining this system. Freedom is not something that can be taken for granted and you often must fight for what you believe. I'm prepared to lead that fight. Please help me.

   Note: To find out the complete story and for a guide on what action you can take, write me personally for my free booklet, "Blow Your Knee Caps Off."

The response literally poured in. Thousands of people responded by tearing out the advertisement and sending it to their congressmen. Others were so outraged that they wrote their congressmen expressing their frustrations with the excesses of the bureaucratic regulatory agencies in general.

The FTC was already under attack by Congress for their excesses, but apparently my advertisement, which later ran in many of the hundreds of magazines that we advertise in regularly, was the catalyst that caused a large outpouring of mail that turned the tide solidly against the FTC. The House passed their FTC bill by 321 to 63 and the Senate passed their bill 77 to 13. The bills were designed to restrict the FTC activities and would give Congress the right to veto any new FTC rule. Finally, in May of 1980 both houses of Congress passed compromise FTC legislation which President Carter signed into law.

The legislation clearly indicated to FTC Chairman Pertschuk and his staff that Congress was very unhappy with their performance. I felt that through the power of my pen I had, in a small way, helped pass that legislation and as a result helped all businessmen.

Before I ran that advertisement, I had practically everybody telling me not to do it—from my attorneys to my family. I was warned that the FTC would triple their efforts against me, which, incidentally, they did. I was told that the FTC would attempt to discredit and smear me in the press. The FTC indeed did just that by issuing a misleading and untruthful press release. And I was told that the FTC would literally try to put me out of business.

With all that unanimous advice not to run the ad, I did it

anyway. I knew I was right. Certainly we had a serious problem and I had technically violated the FTC rule. But the tactics used against me by the FTC were wrong and my confidence to stand up and prevent their continued abuse was motivated by my belief in my Success Forces. I will explain why shortly.

The FTC Revolt advertisement produced thousands of requests for my booklet, "Blow Your Kneecaps Off." The 44-page story of my case included many letters from businessmen and consumers applauding my efforts. In addition to the encouraging letters, I was also getting offers of assistance; many people sent me large dollar contributions which I sent back. I was determined to fight and win my battle with my own resources.

In the several months that followed, we failed to quash the overburdening subpoena which would require us to spend over a year to gather documents. We failed to stop the FTC from continuing to issue their misleading press releases to congressmen who inquired about our case, and we continued to be harassed by the FTC who now were spending thousands of taxpayers' dollars to take revenge against us.

Not one consumer was ever defrauded by JS&A in our eight-year history, and after my public advertising campaign and one and one-half years of investigatory work, the FTC was still unable to prove a case against us. They had to resort to a massive subpoena to examine every record in the hopes of finding something.

My battle with the FTC received a great deal of national publicity and was the subject of numerous editorials and news articles. As the truth slowly emerged, it appeared that the FTC had made a mountain out of a molehill, had gone to excesses to recommend a $100,000 penalty, and then had done a great deal of backtracking to positions more consistent with the way the commission should have operated in the first place.

The case also produced an admission from the FTC that they were unable to go after the fraudulent companies, which was my contention all along. The average comsumer thinks that the FTC protects them from fraud when, in essence, the FTC is only effective against legitimate companies that occasionally may slip.

My battle with the FTC still continues. It will no doubt consume many thousands of dollars and a great deal of my time. The sad part about my battle is the enormous costs taxpayers must also bear. Hopefully my case will give other businessmen the courage to stand up and defend themselves too; if they do, we might be able to reverse the destructive trend in this country. Already Congress is considering legislation that would force a government agency to pay the legal expenses of a person or small business if that party won in court. And the funds would come from the budget of that agency. I have testified before a congressional subcommittee in Washington on this legislation and hopefully it will soon become law.

I am also working on legislation that would help protect others from the government abuses I suffered. I am working with attorneys to present this legislation to Congress in the same forceful way I presented my case to the public. The knowledge that my efforts may help many other Americans and also help keep our country free makes my fight well worth it.

Will I prevail? Will I eventually succeed and prove that one can stand up to the bureaucrats and win? I am convinced I will. I am confident not just because I am right, but because my Success Forces are so intertwined in this story.

Success Force One is honesty. It this case, it is my honesty versus the FTC's dishonesty. The FTC's smear tactics in contrast to the way we've conducted our business and the way we've reacted to their attack.

Success Force Two is failure. To date I have been plagued with a great deal of failure in my battle—the legal fees, the unsuccessful attempt to quash the subpoena, the smear tactics of the FTC, and the ongoing battle. But I know that with each failure I gather another Success Force. I may lose those smaller battles, but I'll win the war.

Success Force Three really says that I should look at my FTC problem as an opportunity. I have an opportunity to contribute to the reform of the FTC and the passing of legislation that will prevent future abuse by regulatory agencies, and I also have the opportunity to show the nation what a solid, honorable, and good company I have built. Without my FTC problem I would never have had that opportunity.

Success Force Four tells me to concentrate my efforts. The temptation to attack all regulatory agencies as opposed to just the FTC was great. Reports of regulatory abuses from practically every regulatory agency have come across my desk, but I have concentrated my efforts on the FTC.

Success Force Five tells me that I had to innovate and that my action had to be different to accomplish my objectives. Simply to copy the established ways of fighting the FTC would have left me in a no-win situation.

Success Force Six tells me that I should clean my desk. When I made my decision to fight the FTC my desk would be clean at the end of the day. But as the battle wore on my desk became cluttered. I knew that in order to be able to clean my desk, I had to delegate even more than I had before and simplify my company's operation. I consequently eliminated some of my previous functions, tightening up our operation, and once again I can clean my desk at the end of the day. The dirty desk was a warning to me that I had to make changes and I made them.

Examine my other success philosophies. I have become an expert on the FTC, I haven't given up, and I am proving that the truth always emerges. I also realized that the FTC attack was a perfect example of success pressures, and knowing this has helped me accept my fate with greater understanding.

"Don't let ego distort good business sense" might be one philosophy that my FTC battle does not seem to follow until you examine the possible results. I felt it made good business sense to fight. If I had agreed to a stiff penalty and our company had received all that bad publicity, our sales and reputation would have suffered. By standing up and fighting the FTC, we have prevented both our sales and our reputation from suffering at all. True, the battle is costing me a great deal in time and money, but in the long run I will look back knowing that it was a good business decision aside from the contribution I will have made to my country.

My FTC battle is only one example of how I am currently using Success Forces to continue to guide me toward success. I use these philosophies every day in my personal and business life. I see over and over how these principles, even when applied against enormous odds, result in eventual success.

And I am convinced that if you too base all your decisions on my six Success Forces, you'll succeed beyond all odds and beyond your expectations.

2
Now Go Get 'em

Where does Joe Sugarman go from here? Certainly I will continue to fight the FTC. There is also so much more I can contribute through writing books that I hope to publish at least one every two years. I plan to continue my seminars both at my Wisconsin estate and throughout the United States and Europe.

I will also continue to write good advertising for JS&A but will turn over the company's reins to Mary Stanke's capable hands and those of her fine staff.

For those of you who would like to get on the JS&A mailing list, just drop us a note addressed to "JS&A Mailing List," One JS&A Plaza, Northbrook, IL 60062. We'll try to keep you informed on our FTC battle, which may drag on for years, and we'll be happy to send you some of our product offerings periodically.

One of my definitions of happiness is "doing what you enjoy and helping others." Hopefully I will be helping others through all of these different activities which I genuinely enjoy doing.

You have learned a great deal about success and failure in this book. I hope reading of my experiences has encouraged you to follow my advice and convinced you that the road to success, although not easy, is easier to reach when you know what really works.

After giving hundreds of speeches and seminars, I have had the thrill of people coming back to me years later telling me how much I changed their lives for the better.

That's what I want to do to your life. I want you to write me a few years from now to tell me how my advice worked for you. In some cases, just a simple thing like cleaning your desk may change your life (I've had people tell me this many times). In some cases, the positive feeling of my book or my "never give up" theory may have made a lasting impression. Whatever thoughts you are left with, and whatever this book does to change your life, I know it will be for the better.

You may not have had a classic failure like my Batman credit card, but if all your failures are looked at as Success Forces you won't reject an opportunity just for the sake of avoiding failure. And remember, one never knows when success will come. Only by attempting something and knowing that failure is a possibility will you even have a chance to succeed.

Success indeed can be yours even beyond your wildest expectations. Believe in my philosophies, realize that the road to success is not easy, and, most important, never give up. Now go get 'em.

APPENDIX

A Collection of Some of JS&A's Historic Advertisements

The Craig Mark II is a direct spin-off of the space-age on-board computers used in the recent Apollo flights. It's integrated solid-state circuitry, built by Texas Instruments, is dependable and designed for a service-free lifetime. In fact the **Craig Corporation guarantees the Mark II for a full year**.

Even under heavy usage the battery will last over 3 years without replacement. After the one year warranty period, any local calculator repair center can change your commercially manufactured rechargeable battery and there are two national Craig service locations that provide "Repair-By-Mail" service. When you purchase your unit—you get the assurance of **complete** calculator service even though the Mark II is designed to be service-free.

As part of a total package the Craig Mark II comes complete with soft imitation leather carrying case, recharger/AC power supply, instruction booklet, one year guarantee and shock resistant plastic carrying case for all the components.

The Mark II was originally introduced last year for $239.95. Thousands of units were sold. The same complete unit is now offered by JS&A for sale through the mail **only** for $179.95 complete with ALL components and with the option to charge the Mark II on your **Master Charge, BankAmericard or American Express** credit card account. PLUS there's a ten-day money back guarantee—you must be **completely satisfied** or return your unit for a full refund.

Please act today during the first day of our national introductory offer. Simply fill out and send in the coupon below and we'll rush your calculator to you by return mail immediately.

ANNOUNCING
THE WORLD'S FINEST PORTABLE CALCULATOR
FOR ONLY $179⁹⁵

It's the most exciting new breakthrough in electronics since the transistor radio!

As a result of new solid state circuitry, the Craig Corporation brings you the Mark II—an **American made** calculator that can add, subtract, multiply, and divide and easily fit into your coat pocket or briefcase. Even more exciting are the features that make it **far more advanced than any comparable calculator** selling for much more.

Features such as the weight—only **twelve ounces**. Such as the **16 digit input** with **8 digit display** or the **constant switch** that permits the multiplication or division by the same number without having to re-enter the constant for each calculation. Such as the **automatic cut-off**—a circuit that automatically dissolves the display and cuts off most of the power if you forget to turn off the calculator. In its cut-off position—the re-chargeable battery will last 40 hours between charges or five hours in constant operation. The letter "L" appears on the display to indicate that your battery needs recharging. And the size—only 1½" thin, 3" wide and 5 ⅛" long.

Features include: **a Clear Entry button** which clears a mistake without erasing your previous calculations; **a limiter system**—a microsecond delay that prevents the accidental entering of two digits simultaneously; **custom keys**—larger keys than a touch-tone telephone—and all packaged in a handsome two-tone housing. It's also easy to learn how to operate the Mark II since a clear, easy-to-follow, instruction booklet is enclosed with each unit.

Even the numbers are new—easy-to-read digits designed for quick recognition.

At the office, the executive can place the Mark II next to his telephone and silently and quickly have all calculations right at his fingertips. Executives who use the Craig as their only

calculator find that the **savings in desk clutter** alone make it worth the modest investment. The Craig Mark II is a precision solid state instrument that can save you time, money, and yet **costs about the same as a good adding machine**. At home, the executive can prepare his notes for an important meeting, balance his family's checking account, or teach the decimal system to his children.

Slip the Mark II into your coat pocket or into your briefcase for a sales visit. Figure out the exact costs, margins or quantities right before your client's eyes. No need ever to postpone a decision because you didn't have the exact figures at hand.

Many of the uses for the Mark II came to us from people who own the calculator:

1. As the ideal device to carry with you when conducting a parts **inventory**.

2. As the perfect **in-flight calculator**. The undisturbed atmosphere of a plane trip is the best time to do your serious financial planning.

3. As the **ideally priced unit** to give **all** your salesmen, purchasing agents, or estimators. Think of the hours saved running to the company calculator.

4. As an important tool for **company presidents**—the most important man in your organization—the man whose decisions should be supported by the finest tools available—like a professional Craig Mark II portable calculator.

The executive, the engineer, the CPA, the surveyor, the insurance adjuster, the salesman, the comptroller, the stockbroker, the buyer—almost anybody in business can certainly use one. The benefits are numerous. The Mark II also makes an excellent gift for the man who has everything.

RUSH ORDER FORM

☐ Please rush me _____ complete Mark II portable electronic calculator(s) @ *$179.95 each with your one year guarantee and 10-day return privilege.

Name _____

Company _____

Address _____

City _____ State _____

Zip _____ Phone _____

☐ Enclosed please find my check for payment in full.

☐ Please charge my Master Charge, BankAmericard or American Express credit card account:

Number _____ Expiration _____
For Master Charge also give four numbers above name.

*Illinois residents subject to 5% sales tax. Add $2.45 for postage and handling. Sorry No C.O.D.'s

Send all orders to:
Order Fulfillment Section
Lock Box 725
Wheeling, Illinois 60090

JS&A
© JS&A, 1972

JS&A *Northbrook, Illinois 60062 ★ (312) 498-6900
¹Speed Skating Capitol of the World

JS&A's first mail order ad, February, 1972

ANNOUNCING

Announcing the
Microma_360
the first real change
in telling time since
time began.

AMERICA'S FIRST
LIQUID CRYSTAL DIGITAL
QUARTZ WATCH

The era of the wristwatch computer has arrived!
The JS&A National Sales Group proudly intro-
duces the Microma 360—the nation's first liquid
crystal digital watch—a solid state computer
that electronically displays the exact time in
digits, 24 hours a day, 365 days a year.

THE ACCURACY OF QUARTZ

Imagine the accuracy of quartz and the miracle
of space-age electronics in one handsome time
piece. The quartz crystal is the latest development in conventional watches. Quartz oscillates
at a precise 32,768 oscillations per second. In
the Microma 360 one micro integrated circuit
containing over 1,000 tiny transistors translates
the precise quartz crystal oscillations into an
equally precise digital readout of time.

NO BUTTON TO PRESS

The Microma 360 has no springs, no hands, no
jewels. There are no moving parts to run down,
wind up or wear out. There is no button to
press since the exact time is constantly shown
on a liquid crystal display screen. To adjust the
Microma 360 you insert a timing fork into the
body of the watch and you advance the time
either by the hour or by the minute—ideal for
frequent travelers who must only change the
hour while passing through time zones.

**PROVEN IN 6 MONTHS
OF CONSUMER TESTING**

Prior to our national introduction approximately 5,000 Microma 360's were sold to consumers over a six month period. Their reaction
was enthusiastic. But more important it proved
that the Microma 360 liquid crystal digital
watch system was accurate, reliable, and indeed
a proven and tested instrument worthy of its
unprecedented two year guarantee.

WATCH THE REACTION

Many people have heard and read about the
liquid crystal digital watch. But few have seen
one. Just wait for the questions and reaction
when your watch is noticed. The 360 is a handsome time piece that says a great deal about
the man who wears one. In addition, its low
introductory price makes it the ideal gift for
the man who has everything.

BATTERY OPERATED

The power source for the Microma 360 is a tiny
commercially available silver oxide battery. The
battery lasts approximately one year and can be
easily changed by your local jeweler.

**THE PRINCIPLE OF
LIQUID CRYSTAL**

Liquid crystal is a clear chemical substance that
turns opaque when charged by currents of electricity. In the Microma display system, small
electrodes are systematically arranged to form
numbers. When a set of preselected electrodes
is charged, numbers appear on the hermetically
sealed watch display. The numbers, which change
every minute, display the time continuously
while a small colon (two dots) oscillates once
every second.

TWO YEAR GUARANTEE

The Microma 360 electronic watch system is
fully guaranteed for two full years. If your
watch does not function properly, mail it to
Microma for repair or replacement—free of
charge. Although the 360 has proven to be
relatively service-free, the ease of mailing a
watch and the prompt Microma service-by-mail
center provide the right combination to satisfy
all your service requirements.

WHO IS MICROMA?

Microma is a subsidiary of Intel Corporation.
Intel is recognized world wide as a leader in
semi-conductor technology and is a well-rated
firm—further assurance that your two year
guarantee is backed by a substantial and reliable firm.

WHO IS JS&A?

The JS&A National Sales Group is one of the
leading national distributors of space-age consumer and business related products. We were
the nation's first company to introduce the
electronic pocket calculator and we have since
pioneered the introduction of many other
widely accepted new products. Despite our size
we insist upon complete customer service and
satisfaction. Our descriptions must be accurate,
our products must represent good value and
you must be completely satisfied. You deal
with people (not computers) and you receive
answers to your letters and prompt refunds if
you so request. The names of our customers

are kept confidential and not sold for mailing
lists. Our insistence on the highest standards of
customer service is your assurance of complete
satisfaction.

IT PAYS TO BUY FROM JS&A

Where can you get the opportunity to be
among the first to buy and wear a totally new
product yet have the option to return it if you
are not absolutely satisfied? JS&A offers you
a two week return privilege—if you are not
absolutely satisfied with the Microma 360—
return it for a prompt refund. It's just that
simple. You can charge your Microma 360 on
your American Express, Diners Club, Bank-
Americard or Master Charge credit card account.
Or send your check for $149.95 plus $2.50 for
postage and handling. If you've been looking
for that special opportunity to own a solid state
digital quartz watch—here it is!

MODESTLY $**149**95
PRICED AT

JS&A NATIONAL SALES GROUP
NORTHBROOK, ILLINOIS 60062 (312) 498-6900

The First Liquid Crystal Digital Watch, January, 1973

The truth about pocket calculators.

What you are about to read may surprise, enlighten or possibly help you. But one thing is clear—you'll have a greater understanding of what is really happening in the calculator industry. There is so much competition, price cutting and look-alike models that today even the most knowledgeable person is confused. We hope this article not only stops the confusion but provides you with the basic knowledge to properly evaluate the best calculator for your requirements. Our first step is to explain the most popular pocket calculator features.

FLOATING & FIXED DECIMAL POINTS

A floating decimal point is one that automatically moves to the correct position in your answer. For example if you divide $100 by 3.25 pounds to determine the cost of one pound, your answer would be $30.76923. The decimal would float five places to the left to give you the exact answer. If you set your calculator to a fixed two position decimal two things would happen. First your answer would drop all but the most significant two digits to the right of the decimal and secondly if your unit had automatic round-off, it would round off the third digit possibly raising the number to the left of it. An answer of $30.77 would therefore result.

CONSTANT FUNCTION

A constant function is a device for locking in a number that you plan to use in successive calculations to save you from constantly re-entering that number. To multiply a series of numbers by 2 you would enter two as the constant. Then when you enter 7, press the equal button, your answer is 14. Press 8, press the equal button and your answer is 16. The 2 remains locked in without its re-entry for each calculation. Most constant functions work on both multiplication and division.

THE DISPLAY

The display is the screen on which the numbers are shown. Displays on pocket calculators vary in size and composition. Each figure is generally composed of seven segments. They are arranged to form the number 8 when they are all illuminated. In some calculators each segment is broken down into three or four fine dots—others in solid lines. As a general rule—the larger the display read-out, the more power is consumed. That is why AC powered desk calculators have a considerably larger display than portable units. Manufacturers have used magnifying lenses for increasing the size of displays without requiring more power thus providing considerably larger read-outs for portable units. The displays most commonly used are the LED (light emitting diode) and more recently, the liquid crystal display. The LED display consists of segments that are self-illuminating whereas liquid crystal is a chemical that turns opaque forming numbers when charged by currents of electricity. The opaque formations are then illuminated by an outside light source. Both systems provide excellent service and legibility.

THE POWER SOURCE

There are two types of portable calculator power sources—rechargeable nickel cadmium batteries or throw-away alkaline batteries. Both have advantages and disadvantages. You can recharge nickel cadmium batteries up to 500 full charges without having to worry about battery replacement. However when you do replace batteries, you pay considerably more for them and they must be changed at a factory service center. In addition, frequent travelers must always bring their AC adapter/chargers with them on trips. With units that are not rechargeable you can throw away the old batteries and slip in new ones yourself.

THE KEYBOARDS AND COMPONENTS

If you think most keyboards are alike—you're right. Actually one manufacturer supplies most of the industry's keyboards. The other components are also supplied by only a few suppliers. In fact, many calculators contain practically the same components with the exception of the outer case.

THE CHIP

The chip in calculator terminology is actually the integrated circuitry that transforms what is entered on a keyboard to an answer on a display. The chip does the job of what formerly took thousands of transistors and is no larger than a dime.

THE COST OF BUILDING A CALCULATOR

The labor cost to assemble the average American made electronic pocket calculator is less than $2. Automation, and American know-how have practically eliminated the labor advantage Japanese manufacturers held for years.

THE TOTAL COST

The most expensive part of a calculator are the components whose costs have remained fairly stable. Components in a rechargeable pocket calculator cost a manufacturer between $60 and $80. He in turn must add his overhead, profit and then sell to a distributor. Based on the above you can see that calculator prices have pretty well bottomed out.

HOW PRICES VARY

Even if prices appear to go lower, look carefully at the features. A Japanese pocket calculator presently being offered for $59.95 has just six digits, no decimal and few other features. That same unit with all the features of a good pocket calculator would cost well over $100. But if all you need are six digits the unit is more than adequate. Another point of confusion is the look-alike unit whose price varies considerably. As an example, North American Rockwell manufactures desk calculators for both Sears and Lloyd's Electronics. Both calculators are very similar. Sears list price is $99.95 with occasional special sales at $89.95. But the Lloyd's unit sells for $69.95. Another example is a popular pocket calculator that sells for $119.95. The UDM-300 manufactured by Universal Data Machine sells for $95. Both have practically the same features with UDM providing a larger display yet there is a $25 price difference. Probably the most spectacular value is the JCE Mark II. With the exception of rechargeable batteries, the calculator has all the features of the popular units, plus an additional two and three position fixed and floating decimal and sells for $75—a full $45 less than current prices.

THE BRAND NAME MAGIC

Of course the magic of a brand name such as Sears might be worth an extra $20 to $40. Appearance also plays an important role. The manufacturer who spends thousands of dollars designing a handsome case can usually demand more for it. Always be careful of calculator close-outs. These units have either been discontinued or didn't sell well in the first place. In the fierce calculator price competition the real winner though has been the consumer . . . if he knows what to look for.

SERVICE

All pocket calculators must be serviced by their respective manufacturers. We know of no manufacturer that operates differently. No matter where you buy, your nearest service depot is generally your mail box. It is therefore important to know that the manufacturer is service conscious and will return your calculator as quickly as possible.

HOW TO DECIDE ON A GOOD CALCULATOR

To intelligently buy a calculator you should first analyze your requirements. It is both foolish and unnecessary to buy a $400 special purpose unit when a $75 calculator would be easier to operate and more practical. There are several ways to determine the type of pocket calculator best suited for your particular needs. Our first suggestion, however, is to forget completely about price. We'll tell you more about that later.

START WITH YOUR EYES

Your most important consideration should be your eyesight. If your eyesight is not perfect or if you use your pocket calculator a great deal, consider first a magnified display. Eye fatigue is not worth the few dollars you'd save by buying a calculator with a tiny display. Your next consideration should be the features. First, do you need a floating decimal? Do you need a constant? If all you do is add dollars and cents—you need neither.

THE POWER CHOICE

Next in importance is your power source. If you use your calculator a great deal in its portable mode consider rechargeable batteries. They generally add to the cost of the calculator but are a practical investment for the really heavy user. If your use is moderate to occasional, throw-away batteries are your best bet. Their ease of replacement makes them quite practical.

THOSE OTHER OPTIONS

Most calculators have a clear entry feature which permits removing a mistaken entry without removing the entire calculation. A battery saving feature causes the display to fade out if the calculator is left undisturbed for ten or more seconds. This help saves the battery power. The sign change feature permits you to change your answer from positive to negative or back to positive at the touch of a button. This is a great convenience if you wish to add or subtract an answer from a chain calculation. Incidentally, a chain calculation is the process of using one or more of the four functions in a series. For example: $2 \times 3 = 6 - 3 = 2 \div 3 = 5$. All pocket calculators do chain calculations yet practically every ad you see mentions this fact.

CHOOSING A SIZE

Most pocket calculators were not designed for your pocket. The most successful units fit into briefcases and measure 1½" x 3" x 5". They are also used frequently as desk units. There is a calculator manufactured by Summit International that actually fits in your pocket. It measures 1¼" x 2¾" x 4" (about the size of a pack of cigarettes). A truly pocket-sized calculator requires more engineering and assembly and generally costs more than the conventional "pocket" calculator. If you really need a unit that takes up the least amount of space or you use your pocket calculator constantly in its portable mode, the extra few dollars are well worth the convenience.

HOW MUCH TO PAY

Now that you understand the different features choose the calculator that best fills your requirements. The price should be your last consideration. It is silly to get less than you require for the sake of saving a few dollars. Don't forget, too, that a pocket calculator is tax deductible if purchased for the purpose of figuring out your income tax.

WHERE AND HOW TO BUY

There are three ways to buy. The first is through a calculator dealer or department store. You have the advantage of personally seeing, touching and making your decision on the spot. There are probably many reputable department stores in your area.

THE DISCOUNTER

The second is the big discounter. In the days when pocket calculators were selling for over $200, this was a good way to buy. Savings were evident. Nowadays with margins so low and the difference between the retail price and the discount price quite small, there is little to gain in buying from a discounter. After all, the discounter who makes just a few dollars on a sale has less of an incentive to issue a refund or provide extra customer service.

THE MAIL ORDER DEALER

The third way to buy is through the mail. A mail order company generally allows you two weeks to decide if you wish to keep a unit. This gives you the opportunity to thoroughly acquaint yourself with your calculator yet have the piece of mind in knowing that you can return it if you are not absolutely satisfied. Mail order companies keep their prices competitive and offer convenient credit card charge options. If you buy a calculator from a company in another state you'll also save on sales tax. Be careful though. Make sure the mail order company is reputable. A check with Dun & Bradstreet or the firm's local Chamber of Commerce can usually get you the information. A good mail order company should be financially strong for prompt refunds, they should answer their mail, and not exploit their customers by selling their names to others for mailing lists.

A NEW WAY TO BUY

The calculator market is confused. Price drops and look alike models have only added to the confusion. JS&A has tried to clear up many of your questions and help you understand what is really happening in the calculator industry. We also hope you consider buying your next calculator from us. We were the nation's first company to introduce the pocket calculator in 1971 and have pioneered the introduction of many widely accepted space-age products. We promise to provide honest descriptions, good value, prompt delivery and the option to return your calculator within two weeks for a prompt refund if you are not absolutely satisfied. In fact we go one step further. To practically eliminate any inconvenience to our customers we have made arrangements with United Parcel Service in practically all but the Western states to pick up your unit at our expense right at your door. JS&A customers are the most pampered in the nation. They have come to expect good service, honest value and the opportunity to be the first to purchase the really exciting new products of our decade. Isn't it time you joined us? **See our calculator ad in today's issue**

JS&A NATIONAL SALES GROUP
628 Michelline, Northbrook, Ill. 60062 (312) 498-6900

One of our most successful calculator ads, January, 1973

SYSTEM 3

The legal recording of phone conversations grows in popularity. Here's how you can save time, money, and improve your efficiency with America's newest business concept.

Tap Your Phone.

A 1971 United States Supreme Court decision clearly made the recording of telephone calls between two parties legal if one of the two parties arranged the recordings. The legal recording of phone conversations thus opened a new concept of business record keeping.

A NEW BUSINESS PRACTICE

You can now record important phone conversations or complicated business discussions and have both a permanent record of the call and an important reference. Very often the inflection and tone in a recording tell more about the conversation than the written facts.

AN ERA OF RESPECTABILITY

Phone tapping has always been associated with espionage, Watergate-type scandals, and controversy. The fact that President Nixon was using this form of record keeping did two things for telephone communication recording. First, it emphasized its legality. Secondly, it paved the way for business use of phone tapping as a new form of business record keeping.

SEVERAL BUSINESS USES

If you have an order taking department think of how much money you'll save in phone bills if you first record the orders and transcribe the results later. In addition you'll always be able to confirm a discrepancy if an error is made. Letters can be dictated and facts can be relayed over the phone quickly and later reviewed or put in written form. Combining your telephone with a good recording device makes sense and saves money.

THREE RECORDING SYSTEMS

The JS&A National Sales Group has developed three recording systems to be used with an induction-type phone pick-up. The pick-up is attached to the telephone head set by means of its suction cup and plugged into any one of three different Craig recording systems with a special cable. There's no installation necessary. The suction cup can be removed in seconds and because nothing is hard-wired to your telephone, there is no way to detect its use during a conversation. Each system has automatic level control to maximize clarity and volume and uses commonly available cassette tapes that range in length from 15 minutes to one hour.

RESPONSIBILITY IS IMPORTANT

With the right to record phone conversations comes an important degree of responsibility. For example, you should always advise your caller that you wish to record the call. Extending this courtesy will be both appreciated by the other party and pave the way to play back the recording if required in the future.

PHONE COMPANY TARIFFS

The telephone company tariffs suggest that a beep tone be placed on the recording at 15 second intervals. Non-compliance with this regulation however violates no law. The telephone

company tariffs are simply the regulations under which the telephone company operates as approved by the Federal Communications Commission. To conform to these regulations, you must go "beep" every 15 seconds during your conversation or obtain an electronic beeping device.

THE FINEST RECORDING EQUIPMENT

JS&A offers the famous Craig line of recording equipment for several reasons. Craig Corporation maintains hundreds of affiliated service locations throughout the country with one probably located in your city. It's always good to know that service is available locally whenever needed or at one of three Craig service-by-mail locations. The line of Craig cassette recorders have always led the industry in value, performance and features—further assurance that the system you purchase is the best recording system for the money. All Craig portable units accept long lasting rechargeable nickel cadmium batteries and the AC adapters act as battery recharging units.

System 1: The Craig portable cassette recorder complete with induction phone pick-up and AC power supply. The unit comes complete with an external remote-control microphone and two cassette tapes. **$59.95**

System 2: The Craig portable cassette recorder with AM/FM radio, built-in condenser microphone and built-in AC adapter. This very attractive portable system can record directly off the AM or FM radio or the induction phone pick-up supplied with each unit. Four free cassettes are supplied. System 2 can also be used as an unobtrusive conference recorder. If you do not have a good AM/FM radio on your desk, the System 2 is a wise investment. **$99.95**

System 3: This is the ultimate in the Craig line of recorders. The System 3 has a built in telephone recording circuit and is a complete dictation and transcribing machine with back spacing and automatic tape counter. Your secretary can transcribe directly from the System 3 just as she does with her current dictation equipment. The System 3 operates on AC current only and comes complete with the telephone pick-up and six cassettes. **$219.95**

The use of phone tapping equipment in legitimate business and record keeping applications makes a great deal of sense. Its constructive and responsible use can save time, money and improve the efficiency of any business.

We hope this ad has opened your eyes to the good aspects of phone tapping. We also hope you consider purchasing your phone tap from us. We promise prompt delivery, good value and the right to return your purchase within two weeks for a prompt refund if you are not absolutely satisfied. We're in business to improve your business. Order a phone tap today.

SYSTEM 2

SYSTEM 1

The induction phone tap is supplied with each system.

JS&A NATIONAL SALES GROUP
628 Michelline, Northbrook, Ill. 60062 (312) 498-6900

Our response to the Watergate Scandal, April, 1973

You own a portable calculator. It has become part of your right arm. It's time to....

Only the man who owns a calculator can fully appreciate all the features and value of the totally new APF Mark VI. And for the man thinking of buying his first unit—your timing is perfect.

APF built the Mark VI to accommodate every important calculator feature in the most practical size. The results combine the newest memory technology and every desired feature in one classic calculator value.

CHAIN MEMORY SAVES TIME

Store the answers from any calculation in a memory bank and automatically obtain the total of those answers. Chain memory then permits you to recall the total stored in the memory and use it in further chain calculations or as a constant ... all without disturbing your original memory total. It's the ultimate achievement in memory logic.

CHAIN MEMORY OPENS NEW POSSIBILITIES

You can now figure out invoice extensions and add or subtract percentage discounts from your total in a few easy steps. You can compute compound interest, cost analysis, expense reports, stock and bond investments—easily and quickly. You'll be amazed at the savings in time. There are no numbers to write down and later re-enter and you enter the minimum amount of data thus avoiding the chance of error. It's like working with two calculators.

NEW PERCENTAGE SYSTEM

The new Mark VI percentage system lets you automatically add or subtract a percentage while still reviewing the percentage amount. For example, to add 5% sales tax to a $50 purchase, enter 50 then the plus key, the number 5 and press the percent key. $2.50 is displayed. Now press the equal key, $52.50 is displayed. In short, you are able to automatically review the percentage amount and by pressing one button, add it to your total. On a conventional calculator it would have taken eleven entries to obtain the same answers.

SUPER LARGE DISPLAY

The large 8 digit green display with zero suppression also has a negative balance sign, an overflow sign, a low battery indicator plus a memory indicator to let you know when you've got something stored in memory. The display also has a 25 second battery saving fade-out. If you forget to turn your unit off, it will automatically conserve 95% of its power.

FOUR FUNCTION CONSTANT

There's a separate four function automatic constant for addition, subtraction, multiplication and division. The constant is automatic. There is no constant switch to turn on and later forget to turn off.

MULTI-PURPOSE KEYS

Three keys serve dual purposes. The MR key (Memory Recall) not only recalls the total in memory but when you press the MR key and then the clear button, your constant appears on the display. The Clear button also acts as a clear entry key and the equals key automatically locks in the constant.

MANY MORE FEATURES

The APF Mark VI also has algebraic logic (you enter the negative sign before the number you wish to subtract as you normally think), a full floating decimal and a limited sign change feature (you can change the sign of numbers entered before you press the equal button).

DESIGNED FOR YOUR DESK OR YOUR BRIEFCASE

The Mark VI complete with batteries weighs only 12½ ounces and measures 1½'' x 4½'' x 6''—just perfect for your briefcase and large enough to make a great all-purpose desk unit. Or give this unique unit as a gift. Its value, features and appearance make it one of today's great product discoveries.

COMPLETE AND SOLIDLY BACKED

Each unit comes complete with 4 AA penlight batteries, an AC power supply, a black soft imitation leather carrying case, and detailed instructions on how to obtain the maximum use from your unit. There's also a one year warranty backed by JS&A. If anything goes wrong with your unit during the first year JS&A will replace it with a brand new unit. After the warranty period APF will repair your unit at any one of their national service-by-mail facilities. Although the Mark VI is built to last, it's still good to know that the manufacturer is service conscience—a very important consideration when you purchase any calculator.

EXPERIENCED MANUFACTURER

APF may have even built your unit. APF is one of the nation's largest manufacturers of private label calculators—calculators labelled with other company's names. They have recently decided to establish their own brand name identity similar to the Bowmar and Texas Instrument trend. So, if you've never heard of them, you will soon. APF is a financially strong public company eager to establish a reputation as America's value and service leader.

A NEW WAY TO BUY

The best way to buy a calculator is to first use it. JS&A's concept of a two week trial period gives you the opportunity to use the APF Mark VI in your home or office under your everyday conditions—not showroom conditions. After two weeks of actual use, you decide whether or not you want to keep it. If you decide to keep your unit, you have the first-hand knowledge that the Mark VI fits your requirements and the peace of mind in knowing that you've made the right choice. If you decide to return it, there's no obligation and you'll receive a prompt and courteous refund. In fact, we go one step further. To practically eliminate any inconvenience to our customers we will pick up your unit in practically all but the Western States, at our expense, right at your door. JS&A customers are the most pampered in the nation. They have come to expect good service, honest value and the opportunity to be the first to purchase the really exciting new products of our decade. Order your Mark VI at no obligation today.

Credit Card Buyers—Call (800) 323-5886 if you wish to phone in your order.

Illinois residents call collect.

Announcing the new APF Mark VI portable memory calculator with the world's most complete feature package.

NATIONAL INTRODUCTORY PRICE

$89.95

RETAIL $129.95

UP-DATE
(TO A MEMORY UNIT)

HANDSOME STYLING

The handsome Mark VI is slightly angled to accommodate desk-top viewing. Its full-thrust keyboard and well-spaced keys make blind entry a breeze.

JS&A NATIONAL SALES GROUP
628 Micheline, Northbrook, Ill. 60062 (312) 498-6900

The JS&A National Sales Group is one of the leading national distributors of electronic calculators and other consumer and business related electronic products. Despite our size we insist upon complete customer service and satisfaction. Our descriptions must be accurate, our products must represent good value and you must be completely satisfied. You deal with people (not computers) and you receive answers to your letters and prompt refunds if you so request. The names of our customers are kept confidential and not sold for mailing lists. Our insistence on the highest standards of customer service is your assurance of complete satisfaction.

Nation's first toll-free credit card order taking ad, October, 1973

A new memory calculator breakthrough means the end of the AC adapter, rechargeable battery and small display and the introduction of a new memory system.

$59⁹⁵

NATIONAL
INTRODUCTORY
PRICE
Sug. Retail $79.95

The world's first ambient light liquid crystal memory pocket calculator—the DataKing 800 manufactured by Rockwell International, can operate for one year on the same set of disposable batteries.

If you've been waiting for the world's most advanced memory calculator—your timing is perfect.

Powered by two inexpensive 9 volt batteries, the 800 will last almost one year on the same set of batteries or ten times longer than even the lowest drain pocket calculators. But there are several other very exciting new feature breakthroughs.

RECHARGEABLE VS DISPOSABLE BATTERIES

It all boils down to convenience vs savings. Rechargeable batteries cost roughly $3.00 per year to power the average pocket calculator. That isn't very expensive. But the calculator owner who wishes to recharge his batteries is always at the mercy of his AC adapter/charger. And the adapter 1) is always subject to malfunction, 2) is often heavier than the calculator and 3) requires AC power to drive it.

If you've ever been on an airplane when your calculator pooped out or if you have been unable to use your calculator because your AC adapter didn't work, you can appreciate the convenience of the disposable battery. But disposable batteries are more expensive—an average of about $4 to $7 to operate the average calculator per year.

The DataKing 800 costs roughly $1.00 per year to operate using readily available 9 volt batteries. Therefore no AC adapter is required nor is one provided.

BIG DISPLAYS VS SMALL DISPLAYS

The display is the biggest consumer of battery power in a calculator. The bigger the display, the more power required to light it. Sunlight can easily overpower the display's light-emitting elements making legibility impossible.

The DataKing 800 has a large easy-to-read liquid crystal display. When small electrodes, arranged to form digits, are charged by microcurrents of electricity, the liquid crystal turns opaque. The resulting numbers must then be illuminated by a light source to provide the contrast needed to read the display. The 800 employs a light-gathering prism that eliminates any need for an internal lighting system and consequently uses a mere fraction of the power required by other conventional calculators. And the brighter the room light, the easier it is to read—even in sunlight.

NEW CLICK-THRUST KEYBOARD

The DataKing 800 has taken the full-thrust keyboard feel and added a click to provide the world's first "click-thrust" keyboard. Not only do you get a very positive data entry feel, but your chance of false entry is greatly minimized by the unique widely-spaced keys.

NEW ACCESS MEMORY SYSTEM

Memory on a calculator is such an important feature that units without it are practically outdated. Memory permits you to store individual numbers or answers to calculations

in a memory bank and then recall the total of those numbers directly onto your display without erasing the total in your memory.

The DataKing 800 has the new access memory. You can now take any number on your display and divide or multiply your memory total by that number—all while retaining that same number on your display. No other calculator has this feature. For example, to add a number to memory, press "M" and the plus key. To divide a number into memory, press "M" and the divide key.

MANY OTHER FEATURES

Now that we've told you all about those revolutionary features, here are some additional qualities that make the DataKing the nation's unquestioned memory leader.

1) Easiest to use Even if the 800 is your first pocket calculator, you'll find it a snap to learn. The algebraic logic (you perform the functions as you think) makes it easy to perform chain calculations. The automatic constants on all six functions require no separate switch to turn on, and there's a separate memory-plus and memory-minus entry system.

> ## COMPARED TO TEXAS INSTRUMENTS
>
> America's leading brand-name calculator is Texas Instruments. TI recently announced their new TI 2550 memory unit for $99.95. That same calculator is now outdated by the introduction of the 800. The TI 2550 uses rechargeable batteries and has a small display and the older chain memory system. Compare price, features, performance and dependability, and you can easily see why the DataKing is America's greatest memory calculator value.

2) The best percentage system To add 5% to a $50 purchase, simply enter $50, then press the plus key, the 5 key and then the percent key. The percentage amount of $2.50 is displayed. Then press the equal key—$52.50 is displayed. In short, you perform percentage problems exactly as you think for both addition, subtraction, multiplication and division.

3) The finest display The large 8-digit liquid crystal display with floating decimal has negative balance and overflow indicators. You can also clear any overflow condition and continue your calculations.

4) Shock resistant The calculator enclosure also eliminates the need for a carrying case and provides a high degree of shock resistance. The display and prism are recessed and thus protected by its rugged high impact resistant case even when accidentally dropped.

5) Handsome styling Rarely do you find so many outstanding features in a highly-styled calculator. The DataKing 800 measures only 1½" x 3½" x 6" and weighs only 10½ ounces. Other features include a clear entry system for memory or mistaken entries, zero suppression, and a full floating decimal.

You are no doubt familiar with Rockwell International and their approach to quality. The DataKing 800 is no exception. Although the 800 was designed to be service-free, your unit is backed by a one year warranty and DataKing's national service-by-mail facility. DataKing, Inc. is a well financed and established company and a leading consumer electronics firm—further assurance that your modest investment is fully protected.

JS&A is so convinced that the 800 is the best memory unit you can buy that we are making the following offer: try the DataKing 800 for a full month. Compare it with every other calculator on the market for features, value, keyboard—whatever. If you are not absolutely convinced that It is the finest calculator value ever offered, return it anytime within that month for a prompt and courteous refund. Truly an unprecedented offer.

EXCHANGE YOUR PRESENT UNIT

Want to exchange your old, outdated calculator for the DataKing 800 without losing too much money? We've got a way. After you are absolutely satisfied with your DataKing 800, send us your outdated unit. JS&A will then send it to a deserving school, non-profit organization, or charitable institution who in turn will send you a letter of appreciation and a certificate acknowledging your contribution. Then use that contribution as a legitimate deduction on your income tax return. You'll be helping somebody in need, while justifying the purchase of the latest calculator technology.

TO ORDER BY MAIL

Each unit is supplied with batteries, warranty card and a thorough instruction booklet. To order the 800 simply send your check for $62.45 ($59.95 plus $2.50 postage and handling Illinois residents add $3.00 sales tax) with your name, address, city, state, and zip code to the address shown below. If you wish to charge the 800 to your Master Charge, BankAmericard, Diners Club, or American Express credit card account, call our toll-free number or send us a brief note listing all numbers on your credit card, expiration date, signature and telephone number. Pick up the phone and order your DataKing 800 at no obligation today.

CREDIT CARD BUYERS CALL:

(800) 323-5880

IN ILLINOIS CALL (312) 498-6900
Lines open until 11pm (C.S.T.)

JS&A
NATIONAL SALES GROUP
4200 Dundee Rd.
Northbrook, Illinois 60062

Our first major national ad campaign, March, 1974

Our biggest loss—$250,000, in March, 1975

Pocket CB

New integrated circuit technology and
a major electronic breakthrough brings you
the world's smallest citizens band transceiver.

SMALL ENOUGH FOR YOUR POCKET

Scientists have produced a personal communications system so small that it can easily fit in your pocket. It's called the PocketCom and it replaces larger units that cost considerably more.

MANY PERSONAL USES

An executive can now talk anywhere with anybody in his office, his factory or job site. The housewife can find her children at a busy shopping center. The motorist can signal for help in an emergency. The salesman, the construction foreman, the traveler, the sportsman, the hobbyist—everybody can use the PocketCom—as a pager, an intercom, a telephone or even a security device.

LONG RANGE COMMUNICATIONS

The PocketCom's range is limited only by its 100 milliwatt power and the number of metal objects between units or from a few blocks in the city to several miles on a lake. Its receiver is so sensitive, that signals several miles away can be picked up from stronger citizens band base or mobile stations.

VERY SIMPLE OPERATION

To use the PocketCom simply turn it on, extend the antenna, press a button to transmit, and release it to listen. And no FCC license is required to operate it. The PocketCom has two Channels—channel 14 and an optional second channel. To use the second channel, plug in one of the 22 other citizens band crystals and slide the channel selector to the second position. Crystals for the second channel cost $7.95 and can only be ordered after receipt of your unit.

The PocketCom components are equivalent to 112 transistors whereas most comparable units contain only twelve.

A MAJOR BREAKTHROUGH

The PocketCom's small size results from a breakthrough in the solid state device that made the pocket calculator a reality. Mega scientists took 112 transistors, integrated them on a micro silicon wafer and produced the world's first transceiver linear integrated circuit. This major breakthrough not only reduced the size of radio components but improved their dependability and performance. A large and expensive walkie talkie costing several hundred dollars might have only 12 transistors compared to 112 in the Mega PocketCom.

BEEP-TONE PAGING SYSTEM

You can page another PocketCom user, within close range, by simply pressing the PocketCom's call button which produces a beep tone on the other unit if it has been left in the standby mode. In the standby mode the unit is silent and can be kept on for weeks without draining the batteries.

SUPERIOR FEATURES

Just check the advanced PocketCom features now possible through this new circuit breakthrough: 1) Incoming signals are amplified several million times compared to only 100,000 times on comparable conventional systems. 2) Even with a 60 decibel difference in signal strength, the unit's automatic gain control will bring up each incoming signal to a maximum uniform level. 3) A high squelch sensitivity (0.7 microvolts) permits noiseless operation without squelching weak signals. 4) Harmonic distortion is so low that it far exceeds EIA (Electronic Industries Association) standards whereas most comparable systems don't even meet EIA specification. 5) The receiver has better than one microvolt sensitivity.

EXTRA LONG BATTERY LIFE

The PocketCom has a light-emitting diode low-battery indicator that tells you when your 'N' cell batteries require replacement. The integrated circuit requires such low power that the two batteries, with average use, will last weeks without running down.

EXECUTIVES	POLICE	MOTORISTS
SHOPPERS	HIKERS	FOREMEN

The PocketCom can be used as a pager, an intercom, a telephone or even a security device.

MULTIPLEX INTERCOM

Many businesses can use the PocketCom as a multiplex intercom. Each employee carries a unit tuned to a different channel. A stronger citizens band base station with 23 channels is used to page each PocketCom. The results: an inexpensive and flexible multiplex intercom system for large construction sites, factories, offices, or farms.

NATIONAL SERVICE

The PocketCom is manufactured exclusively for JS&A by Mega Corporation. JS&A is America's largest supplier of space-age products and Mega Corporation is a leading manufacturer of innovative personal communication systems—further assurance that your modest investment is well protected. The

The PocketCom measures approximately ¾" x 1½" x 5½" and easily fits into your shirt pocket. The unit can be used as a personal communications link for business or pleasure.

PocketCom should give you years of trouble-free service, however, should service ever be required, simply slip your 5 ounce Pocket-Com into its handy mailer and send it to Mega's prompt national service-by-mail center. It is just that easy.

GIVE IT A REAL WORKOUT

Remember the first time you saw a pocket calculator? It probably seemed unbelievable. The PocketCom may also seem unbelieveable so we give you the opportunity to personally examine one without obligation. Order only two units on a trial basis. Then really test them. Test the range, the sensitivity, the convenience. Test them under your everyday conditions and compare the PocketCom with larger units that sell for several hundred dollars.

After you are absolutely convinced that the PocketCom is indeed that advanced product breakthrough, order your additional units, crystals or accessories on a priority basis as one of our established customers. If, however, the PocketCom does not suit your particular requirements perfectly, then return your units within ten days after receipt for a prompt and courteous refund. You cannot lose. Here is your opportunity to test an advanced space-age product at absolutely no risk.

A COMPLETE PACKAGE

Each PocketCom comes complete with mercury batteries, high performance Channel 14 crystals for one channel, complete instructions, and a 90 day parts and labor warranty. To order by mail, simply mail your check for $39.95 per unit (or $79.90 for two) plus $2.50 per order for postage, insurance and handling to the address shown below. (Illinois residents add 5% sales tax). But don't delay.

Personal communications is the future of communications. Join the revolution. Order your PocketComs at no obligation today.

$39⁹⁵ NATIONAL INTRODUCTORY PRICE

Our biggest success—250,000 units starting in September, 1975

First electronic blood pressure unit, November, 1977

Burglar Alarm Breakthrough

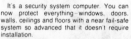

A new computerized burglar alarm requires no installation and protects your home or business like a thousand dollar professional system.

The Midex security computer looks like a handsome stereo system component and measures only 4"x 10¹₂"x 7".

It's a security system computer. You can now protect everything—windows, doors, walls, ceilings and floors with a near fail-safe system so advanced that it doesn't require installation.

The Midex 55 is a new motion-sensing computer. Switch it on and you place a harmless invisible energy beam through more than 5,000 cubic feet in your home. Whenever this beam detects motion, it sends a signal to the computer which interprets the cause of the motion and triggers an extremely loud alarm.

The system's alarm is so loud that it can cause pain—loud enough to drive an intruder out of your home before anything is stolen or destroyed and loud enough to alert neighbors to call the police.

The powerful optional blast horns can also be placed outside your home or office to warn your neighbors.

Unlike the complex and expensive commercial alarms that require sensors wired into every door or window, the Midex requires no sensors nor any other additional equipment other than your stereo speakers or an optional pair of blast horns. Its beam actually penetrates walls to set up an electronic barrier against intrusion.

NO MORE FALSE ALARMS

The Midex is not triggered by noise, sound, temperature or humidity—just motion—and since a computer interprets the nature of the motion, the chances of a false alarm are very remote.

An experienced burglar can disarm an expensive security system or break into a home or office through a wall. Using a Midex system there is no way a burglar can penetrate the protection beam without triggering the loud alarm. Even if the burglar cuts off your power, the four-hour rechargeable battery pack will keep your unit triggered, ready to sense motion and sound an alarm.

DEFENSE AGAINST PEEPING TOMS

By pointing your unit towards the outdoors from your bedroom and installing an outside speaker, light, or alarm, your unit can sense a peeping Tom and frighten him off. Pets are no problem for the Midex. Simply put them in one section of the house and concentrate the beam in another.

When the Midex senses an intruder, it remains silent for 20 seconds. It then sounds the alarm until the burglar leaves. One minute

after the burglar leaves, the alarm shuts off and resets, once again ready to do its job. This shut-off feature, not found on many expensive systems, means that your alarm won't go wailing all night long while you're away. When your neighbors hear it, they'll know positively that there's trouble.

PROFESSIONAL SYSTEM

Midex is portable so it can be placed anywhere in your home. You simply connect it to your stereo speakers or attach the two optional blast horns.

Operating the Midex is as easy as its installation. To arm the unit, you remove a specially coded key. You now have 30 seconds to leave your premises. When you return, you enter and insert your key to disarm the unit. You have 20 seconds to do that. Each key is registered with Midex, and that number is kept in their vault should you ever need a duplicate. Three keys are supplied with each unit.

As an extra security measure, you can leave your unit on at night and place an optional panic button by your bed. But with all its optional features, the Midex system is complete, designed to protect you, your home and property just as it arrives in its wellprotected carton.

The Midex 55 system is the latest electronic breakthrough by Solfan Systems, Inc.—a company that specializes in sophisticated professional security systems for banks and high security areas. JS&A first became acquainted with Midex after we were burglarized. At the time we owned an excellent security system, but the burglars went through a wall that could not have been protected by sensors. We then installed over $5,000 worth of the Midex commercial equipment in our warehouse. When Solfan Systems announced their intentions to market their units to consumers, we immediately offered our services.

COMPARED AGAINST OTHERS

In a recent issue of a leading consumer publication, there was a complete article written on the tests given security devices which were purchased in New York. The Midex 55 is not available in New York stores, but had it been compared, it would have been rated tops in space protection and protection against false alarms—two of the top criteria used to evaluate these systems. Don't be confused. There is no system under $1,000 that provides you with the same protection.

YOU JUDGE THE QUALITY

Will the Midex system ever fail? No product is perfect, but judge for yourself. All components used in the Midex system are of aerospace quality and of such high reliability that they pass the military standard 883 for thermal shock and burn-in. In short, they go through the same rugged tests and controls used on components in manned spaceships.

Each component is first tested at extreme

tolerances and then retested after assembly. The entire system is then put under full electrical loads at 150 degrees Fahrenheit for an entire week. If there is a defect, these tests will cause it to surface.

PEOPLE LIKE THE SYSTEM

Wally Schirra, a scientist and former astronaut, says this about the Midex 55. "I know of no system that is as easy to use and provides such solid protection to the homeowner as the Midex. I would strongly recommend it to anyone. I am more than pleased with my unit."

Many more people can attest to the quality of this system, but the true test is how it performs in your home or office. That is why we provide a one month trial period. We give you the opportunity to see how fail-safe and easy to operate the Midex system is and how thoroughly it protects you and your loved ones.

Use the Midex for protection while you sleep and to protect your home while you're away or on vacation. Then after 30 days, if you're not convinced that the Midex is nearly fail-safe, easy to use, and can provide you with a security system that you can trust, return your unit and we'll be happy to send you a prompt and courteous refund. There is absolutely no obligation. JS&A has been serving the consumer for over a decade—further assurance that your investment is well protected.

To order your system, simply send your check in the amount of **$199.95** (Illinois residents add 5% sales tax) to the address shown below. Credit card buyers may call our toll-free number below. There are no postage and handling charges. By return mail you will receive your system complete with all connections, easy to understand instructions and a one year limited warranty. If you do not have stereo speakers, you may order the optional blast horns at **$39.95** each, and we recommend the purchase of two.

With the Midex 55, JS&A brings you: 1) A system built with such high quality that it complies with the same strict government standards used in the space program. 2) A system so advanced that it uses a computer to determine unauthorized entry, and 3) A way to buy the system, in complete confidence, without even being penalized for postage and handling charges if it's not exactly what you want. We couldn't provide you with a better opportunity to own a security system than right now.

Space-age technology has produced the ultimate personal security computer. Order your Midex 55 at no obligation, today.

JS&A NATIONAL SALES GROUP

Dept. WJ   One JS&A Plaza
Northbrook, Ill. 60062   (312) 564-9000
Call TOLL-FREE 800 323-6400
In Illinois Call ...... (312) 498-6900
ⓒ JS&A Group, Inc.,1978

First mass-marketed security system, June, 1977

OK WORLD, WE'RE READY

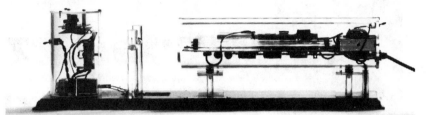

Laser Beam Mousetrap

"Build a better mousetrap and the world will beat a path to your door."

This is the story of two very unusual products. The first is a marketing phenomenon and the second a marketing experiment.

THE MARKETING EXPERIMENT

The marketing experiment has been designed to prove a well-known marketing premise. It was once said that if you build a better mousetrap, the world would beat a path to your door. So American scientists have developed the world's first laser beam mousetrap—a space-age triumph using the latest laser technology and American scientific genius.

If the premise is correct, the world should recognize this outstanding achievement and beat a path to our door. There is no technologically more advanced mousetrap in the world. If the premise is incorrect, then this marketing experiment will certainly prove it.

A REAL LASER

The laser beam mousetrap consists of a functioning laboratory laser with an ingenious wire hammer solenoid-activated spring mechanism. The entire system is mounted on an attractive polished walnut base which can be handsomely displayed in any office, board room, or rodent-infested area.

The laser is of the helium neon variety radiating in red at a wavelength of 6,328 ångstroms with one half milliwatts of power. All mechanisms are safely housed in a transparent acrylic container.

To activate the mousetrap, you place peanut butter in a small circular container located in the center of the trap. The laser beam is deflected down to the peanut butter, keeping it illuminated while the odor stays fresh. The wire hammer device is then cocked and held in position by a solenoid.

As the mouse nibbles the peanut butter, the laser beam is interrupted and a photo diode senses the mouse's presence and releases the spring-loaded hammer wire. Kerplow!

The mouse is then conveniently and rather rapidly put to rest.

The laser beam mousetrap is offered for only $1500 complete with a jar of peanut butter, complete instructions and a one year warranty—all during our special national introductory offer.

THE MARKETING PHENOMENON

The same company that invented the laser beam mousetrap is also in the midst of a marketing phenomenon.

The Holex Corporation has pioneered in the commercial application of laser technology and has done numerous laser experiments to create three-dimensional images on flat pieces of glass. When Holex placed these glass images in a gold-plated frame, not only did it make an unusual piece of jewelry, but it appeared to glow in iridescent colors enhancing the three-dimensional effect and creating an optical sensation for those who saw it.

Holex felt that laser pendant jewelry might make an interesting consumer item. To test it, they produced a few sample pieces which they sold for $50 each in a New York City jewelry store—well below their actual cost.

The hammer-wire mechanism is cocked and held in place by the solenoid.

The first production run quickly sold out. So did the second. It was then that Holex contacted JS&A and offered us the opportunity to offer the world's first mass-produced laser pendant in a large production run.

A small test run flyer was sent out to a selected group of our customers offering the pendant for $20. It received the biggest response we've ever received for any single product in our history. In addition, for every pendant we sold, we received an average of three reorders.

We called the results of our program a marketing phenomenon. Normally, a well-accepted product has a 10% reorder rate, but a 300% reorder rate was really an incredible statement about this exciting new product.

To capitalize on this marketing phenomenon, JS&A has made available its most popular two pendants, one called "Watch Movement," showing the inside workings of a watch, and the second, "Gold Dollar," showing a gold dollar good luck charm. Both objects come complete with necklace chain and gift box—all for the same low price of $20.

The pendants make great Mother's Day gifts, a gift for your employees, or a gift for anyone to whom you want to give a token of your appreciation or affection. It's truly an unusual and well-accepted gift idea that draws admiring glances and many compliments.

Laser technology is a relatively new technology. Its effects are being felt every day as new and more advanced uses for this science are being developed. JS&A is proud to introduce two of the newest technologies.

AN UNUSUAL OFFER

The laser beam mousetrap sells for $1500 and comes complete with peanut butter, instructions, and one year warranty. The laser pendants are offered for $20 each. (Illinois residents add 5% sales tax.) There are no postage and handling charges for either purchase. Credit card buyers may call our toll-free number to order. There is also a ten day trial period for each item. If you are not absolutely satisfied with your purchase, return it within ten days for a prompt and courteous refund. You can't lose.

PARTICIPATE WITH US

For each of you who participate with us and order either a laser pendant or a mousetrap, we will send you, three months after your purchase, a report on the results of our marketing experiment. We will tell you how many laser beam mousetraps were sold and our conclusions. Won't you join us and order either product at no obligation today?

The Laser Pendants are 1¼ inches in diameter and come complete with matching metal chain and gift box. When ordering, specify "Watch Works" or "Gold Dollar."

Our biggest dud—we didn't sell one, April, 1977

NEW CONCEPT

Dial Free

The Supreme Court of the United States, GTE, and a major new telephone breakthrough open the door to new consumer savings.

The new pocket-sized Flip-Phone T.M. telephone from GTE will save consumers millions.

The Flip-Phone flips open to reveal the keyboard and the privacy switch.

America's phone system is the world's greatest. No country can compare. But what has made our phone system even greater is the recent Supreme Court decision that permits consumers to plug in their own phones – phones that they can buy themselves.

We are now free to choose which phone we want to plug in. And that creates competition and competition usually results in lower prices, innovative products, and better service.

We now do have lower prices and a very exciting new product which we have selected as the best example of the new telephone ownership decision. The big breakthrough, however, is not the product itself, but an attitude. But more on that later.

THE NEW PHONE

It's called the Flip-Phone and it's manufactured by General Telephone and Electronics (GTE), a supplier of phones to other telephone companies. The Flip-Phone is a major breakthrough described by GTE as "the most advanced new telephone in the last ten years."

Most telephones contain a handset (the thing you talk over) and the base (where the electronics are located). GTE was able to condense the electronics on tiny integrated circuits which have been placed in the handset making the telephone base unnecessary.

THE MISSING MOUTHPIECE

Telephones contain large magnets which add to the handset's weight. The new Flip-Phone uses a very small and lightweight condenser microphone so sensitive that it picks up your voice even better than the conventional phone with its large mouthpiece.

And then there's the dial itself. It's gone. And in its place is a keyboard – a device that lets you tap out numbers without having to dial. This is a major breakthrough for three reasons: 1) It is a very fast way to dial. 2) It works on telephone systems that do not even accept *touch-tone* dialing, and 3) Even if you owned a *touch-tone* phone, you could plug in the Flip-Phone and not be charged for the extra service. You actually are able to push-button dial for free.

We're now going to tell you a few of the other new features, but the really big breakthrough, we'll tell you about later.

Privacy Switch Just flip a switch and you turn off the phone's ringer. It's ideal when you go to sleep, at dinner, or when you want privacy.

New Ring Most telephone ringers sound the same. The Flip-Phone emits an electronic warbling sound – a very pleasant tone.

New Cord Even the cord on the Flip-Phone is different. It's 14 feet long – twice as long as a

conventional cord. One end is coiled and the other is straight. You can use either end to connect to your phone while the other end connects to the wall. And if your cord gets twisted, dirty, or plain chewed up, just unplug it and put in a new one. It's just that easy.

Low Cost The Flip-Phone costs only $49.95 which means that it will pay for itself quickly – not only in convenience, but with savings of up to $4 a month in some cities. When you determine the true cost of telephone ownership, you compare costs over a five-year period. In five years even a $2.00 telephone charge per month equals $120 or over twice the cost of the Flip-Phone telephone.

Small Size The Flip-Phone is the size of a large stapler. When you pick it up, a panel flips open revealing the touch-pad dial, and the panel acts as a guide to funnel your voice to the condenser microphone. The Flip-Phone is only 2¼" wide x 1¼" high x 7" long and weighs only seven ounces.

THE BIG BREAKTHROUGH

The really big breakthrough is not the Flip-Phone. GTE did indeed spend several million dollars developing the item, and we feel that it will be the single most important phone in America within a few short years. No, the real breakthrough is the change in attitude of the telephone companies. We can remember when even putting a telephone answering unit on your line almost caused you to lose your phone service.

TIMES HAVE CHANGED

The telephone companies are now so cooperative that they deserve great respect. After all, they lose money every time you plug in your own phone, so their cooperation in light of their loss must be commended.

And they have made connecting your phone easier than ever before. Remember those big four-pronged jacks? Now there's a small connector which the phone company installs for around $15 (depending on your city). Where can you find an electrician or a plumber to come to your home for $15?

If you want to plug in your own phones and don't have the modular receptacles, just call the phone company and see how courteous they are. Tell them that you are ordering a phone with a ringer equivalent of 1.2B, an FCC registration number of AB898Y-62927-TE-R, and that you want them to remove your phones and stop charging you for them. That's all you have to do.

They'll promptly send a repairman to your home to attach the modular connector for the Flip-Phone. If you already have a four-pronged

jack you can use a modular adapter and avoid the service charge completely.

Then order a Flip-Phone from GTE. They'll be in most retail stores sometime this year. Or avoid the wait and order one now directly from us. We were the first major national distributor of the Flip-Phone and have already delivered thousands to homes throughout the country.

Put one in your kitchen, in your study, in your children's room, or even in your office. You'll appreciate the convenience and savings.

If service is ever required, GTE has a prompt service-by-mail center. About the only thing that goes wrong with today's phones is the tangled cord. With the Flip-Phone telephone, you just unplug the old cord and plug in the new one. It's just that simple.

A PERSONAL TEST

We urge you to at least give the Flip-Phone a personal test right in your own home under your everyday conditions. Order one from JS&A under our 30-day trial period. Plug it in. See how easy it is to dial numbers by pressing buttons. See how good it looks and how little space it takes up. Find out how much better you sound at the other end. Then within 30 days decide if you want to keep it. If you are not convinced that the GTE Flip-Phone is a very good investment, return your phone and we'll promptly refund your money – every penny including our $2.50 postage and handling charge. You can't lose.

To order your Flip-Phone, simply send your check for **$49.95** plus $2.50 for postage and handling to the address shown below. (Illinois residents, please add 5% sales tax.) Or credit card buyers may call our toll-free number.

The Flip-Phone comes in four colors: white, yellow, brown and beige. Just specify the color, and we'll send you the phone, cord, 90-day limited warranty, and simple instructions. If you have four-pronged jacks, just order the adapter plugs for $2 each.

Why not act ahead of the crowd and order an exciting new space-age way to cut down on your phone bills? Order your Flip-Phone at no obligation, today.

Touch-tone is a registered trademark of AT&T

JS&A PRODUCTS THAT THINK

Dept.OM   One JS&A Plaza
Northbrook, Ill. 60062   (312) 564-7000
Call TOLL-FREE **800 323-6400**
In Illinois Call .... **(312) 564-7000**

© JS&A Group, Inc.,1979

The first successful telephone product, September, 1978

CHESS DIPLOMACY

Soviet Challenge

This is the computer that may change the course of chess playing history.

Can an American chess computer beat the Soviet Chess Champion? A Confrontation between American space-age technology and a Soviet psychological weapon.

The Soviet Union regards chess as a psychological weapon, not just a game. It is a symbol of communism's cultural struggle with the West.

So when Russian Anatoli Karpov competed against the Russian Defector, Victor Korchnoi, he had the entire Soviet Union's resources at his disposal, including a hypnotist and neuro-psychologist.

Karpov won. And with it the world's undisputed chess championship. Karpov however, has never confronted American space-age technology and in particular JS&A's new Chess Computer.

So representatives of JS&A met with Karpov's representatives in Hong Kong in an effort to arrange a match between the Soviet Champion and the JS&A Chess Computer.

It wasn't easy negotiating with the Soviets. We offered them a $50,000 guarantee against royalties from the sales of our chess computers. But negotiations broke down.

Was the Soviet delegation afraid that American space-age technology would win? Were the Soviets fearful of negative publicity if Karpov lost to a $100 computer? Or were they fearful of a circus-type atmosphere that would degrade their prestige, even if he won?

Honestly, we don't know. We do know that our offer is still open, but we suspect Karpov will not accept.

Why did we challenge Karpov? Simple. We thought that having Karpov play against our computer would focus world-wide attention on our product. This attention would increase its sales and win or lose, we would sell more computers.

We had to sell more computers. We wanted to sell our unit for $100 even though it compares with units that sell for more than $300. But we had to do two things in order to sell our unit for $100. First, we had to manufacture it in Hong Kong where labor costs are very low. Secondly, we had to sell large quantities.

SOPHISTICATED DESIGN

The JS&A Chess Computer is designed to look several moves ahead to determine its next move. When we first designed it, it played five levels of chess. Level one was for beginners and as you played against the computer, you could increase its level of difficulty until the computer became more of a challenge. Level five was quite a challenge.

We thought we had the ultimate unit with five levels, until we developed our most sophisticated unit which has six levels. With six levels and all its previous features, the system is now a challenge for any Soviet Chess Champion.

The JS&A Chess Computer is a small unit that comes without a board or chess pieces. We felt that most players prefer their own board and pieces anyway.

LIKE PLAYING KARPOV

The system is the perfect way to sharpen your chess skills. It not only has six different skill levels, but if you are playing against the computer at level two and you are beating it, you can switch the unit to level six. It's like having Karpov as your new opponent – right during mid game.

To play against the computer, you enter your move on the unit's keyboard. You then wait until the computer examines all its options and selects its move. You then move the computer's chess piece to correspond with its request as shown on the display. A board layout is provided to show you where each chess piece should be moved.

SHARPEN SKILLS

If you already play chess, the JS&A unit provides a new chess dimension. If you haven't played chess, the system is a good way to learn and sharpen your skills.

The JS&A Chess Computer measures only 2⅛" x 4⅞" x 8⅞" and weighs just a few ounces, so if service is ever required you can slip it in its handy mailer and send it back to our prompt service-by-mail center. Service should never be required, but it is reassuring to know that service is an important consideration in this program.

JS&A is America's largest single source of space-age products – further assurance that your modest investment is well protected.

We suggest you order a JS&A Chess Computer on our 30 day trial period. Play against it. Raise or lower the level as you play and watch how the computer's personality can change right in mid-game – from a tough competitor to a push over.

TEST LEVEL SIX

Test our level six and see if you'd have much of a chance against the Soviet Champion Karpov. Then, after you've really given it a workout, decide if you want to keep it. If not, you may return your unit for a prompt and courteous refund, including your $2.50 postage and handling charge. There is no risk. Each JS&A Chess Computer comes complete with instructions and an AC adapter (no batteries are required).

To order your JS&A Chess Computer, send your check for **$99.95** plus $2.50 for postage and handling (Illinois residents please add 5% sales tax) to the address below or credit card buyers may call our toll-free number below.

The Soviet Union may have the World's Chess Champion, but JS&A has a very powerful Chess Computer and something the Soviets don't have – a pretty good advertising department.

Why not order a JS&A Chess Computer at no obligation, today.

JS&A PRODUCTS THAT THINK

Dept.WJ   One JS&A Plaza
Northbrook, Ill. 60062   (312) 564-7000
Call TOLL-FREE **800 323-6400**
In Illinois Call .... **(312) 564-7000**
©JS&A Group, Inc.,1978

Typical of the creative JS&A advertising approach, November, 1978

The Bone Fone stereo radio, November, 1979

FTC Revolt

You've heard of the tax revolt. It's about time for an FTC revolt. Here's my story and why we've got to stop federal bureaucratic regulation.

By Joseph Sugarman.
President, JS&A Group, Inc.

My story is only one example of how the FTC is harassing small businesses but I'm not going to sit back and take it.

I'm pretty lucky. When I started my business in my basement eight years ago. I had little more than an idea and a product.

The product was the pocket calculator. The idea was to sell it through advertisements in national magazines and newspapers.

Those first years in the basement weren't easy. But, we worked hard and through imaginative advertising and a dedicated staff, JS&A grew rapidly to become well recognized as an innovator in electronics and marketing.

THREE BLIZZARDS

In January of 1979, three major blizzards struck the Chicago area. The heaviest snowfall hit Northbrook, our village - just 20 miles north of Chicago.

Many of our employees were stranded unable to get to our office where huge drifts made travel impossible. Not only were we unable to reach our office, but our computer totally broke down leaving us in even deeper trouble.

But we fought back. Our staff worked around the clock and on weekends. First, we processed orders manually. We also hired a group of computer specialists, rented outside computer time, employed a computer service bureau, and hired temporary help to feed this new computer network. We never gave up. Our totally dedicated staff and the patience of many of our customers helped us through the worst few months in our history. Although there were many customers who had to wait over 30 days for their parcels, every package was eventually shipped.

WE OPENED OUR DOORS

During this period, some of our customers called the FTC (Federal Trade Commission) to complain. We couldn't blame them. Despite our efforts to manually notify our customers of our delays, our computer was not functioning making the task extremely difficult.

The FTC advised JS&A of these complaints. To assure the FTC that we were a responsible company, we invited them to visit us. During their visit we showed them our computerized microfilm system which we use to back up every transaction. We showed them our new dual computer system (our main system and a backup system in case our main system ever failed again). And, we demonstrated how we were able to locate and trace every order. We were very cooperative, allowing them to look at every document they requested.

The FTC left. About one week later, they

called and told us that they wanted us to pay a $100,000 penalty for not shipping our products within their 30-day rule. (The FTC rule states that anyone paying by check is entitled to have their purchase shipped within 30 days or they must be notified and given the option to cancel.)

NOT BY CONGRESS

The FTC rule is not a law nor a statute passed by Congress, but rather a rule created by the FTC to strengthen their enforcement powers. I always felt that the rule was intended to be used against companies that purposely took advantage of the consumer. Instead, it appears that the real violators, who often are too difficult to prosecute, get away while JS&A, a visible and highly respected company that pays taxes and has contributed to our free enterprise system, is singled out. I don't think that was the intent of the rule.

And when the FTC goes to court, they have the full 'resources of the US Government. Small, legitimate businesses haven't got a chance.

We're not perfect. We do make mistakes. But if we do make a mistake, we admit it, accept the responsibility, and then take whatever measures necessary to correct it. That's how we've built our reputation.

BLOW YOUR KNEE CAPS OFF

Our attorneys advised us to settle. As one attorney said, "It's like a bully pulling out a gun and saying, 'If you don't give me a nickel, I'll blow your knee caps off.'" They advised us that the government will subpoena thousands of documents to harass us and cause us great inconvenience. They warned us that even if we went to court and won, we would end up spending more in legal fees than if we settled.

To settle would mean to negotiate a fine and sign a consent decree. The FTC would then issue a press release publicizing their victory.

At first we tried to settle. We met with two young FTC attorneys and agreed in principle to pay consumers for any damages caused them. But there were practically no damages, just a temporary computer problem, some late shipments, and some bad weather. The FTC then issued a massive subpoena requesting documents that will take us months to gather and which we feel was designed to harass or force us to accept their original $100,000 settlement request.

Remember, the FTC publicizes their actions. And the higher the fine, the more the

publicity and the more stature these two attorneys will have at the FTC.

If this all sounds like blackmail - that's just what it appeared to be to us.

We did ship our products late - something we've admitted to them and which we publicly admit here, but we refuse to be blackmailed into paying a huge fine at the expense of our company's reputation - something we've worked hard eight years to build.

We're not a big company and we realize it would be easier to settle now at any cost. But we're not. If this advertisement can attract the attention of Congressmen and Senators who have the power to stop the harassment of Americans by the FTC, then our efforts will be well spent.

ALL AMERICANS AFFECTED

Federal regulation and the whims of a few career-building bureaucrats is costing taxpayers millions, destroying our free enterprise system, affecting our productivity as a nation and as a result is lowering everybody's standard of living.

I urge Congressmen, Senators, businessmen and above all, the consumer to support legislation to take the powers of the FTC from the hands of a few unelected officials and bring them back to Congress and the people.

I will be running this advertisement in hundreds of magazines and newspapers during the coming months. I'm not asking for contributions to support my effort as this is my battle, but I do urge you to send this advertisement to your Congressmen and Senators. That's how you can help.

America was built on the free enterprise system. Today, the FTC is undermining this system. Freedom is not something that can be taken for granted and you often must fight for what you believe. I'm prepared to lead that fight. Please help me.

Note: To find out the complete story and for a guide on what action you can take, write me personally for my free booklet, "Blow your knee caps off."

JS&A PRODUCTS THAT THINK

One JS&A Plaza, Northbrook, Ill. 60062
© JS&A Group, Inc., 1980

The FTC ad, November, 1979

Index

University of Illinois, 10
University of Miami, 10–11

W

Wagley, Harvey, 72–73
Wall Street Journal
    advertisements, 76–77, 85, 93,
    179
Washington Post advertisements,
    155, 179
Watergate scandal, impact of on
    JS&A, 84–93
Watergate scandal game, 87–93
Wayne, John, 4–6
WCFL Radio, 30, 39, 44
Whitney, Emerson, 54–55
Wiener, Dr. Norbert, 165
WINZ Radio, 13

Y

Yalowitz, Edward, 48